FAMOUS EDINBURGH CRIMES

ROSS MACDONALD

Illustrated by John Mackay

Lang**Syne**

PUBLISHING

WRITING *to* REMEMBER

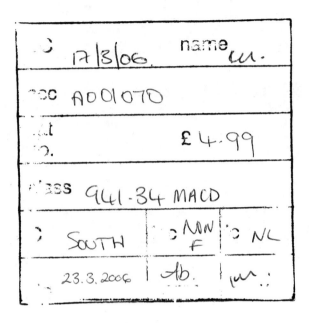

Handwritten library card:

17/3/06, name *uu.*

AOOIO7O

£4.99

941.34 MACD

SOUTH   MON F   NL

23.3.2006   Ab.   uu.

Lang**Syne**

PUBLISHING

WRITING *to* REMEMBER

Strathclyde Business Centre
120 Carstairs Street, Glasgow G40 4JD
Tel: 0141 554 9944 Fax: 0141 554 9955
E-mail: scottishmemories@aol.com
www.scottish-memories.co.uk

Printed by JSB Print, Glasgow
Design and artwork by Roy Boyd and David Braysher
© Lang Syne Publishers Ltd 2003
ISBN 0-946264-18-X

contents

Foreword

The day Edinburgh's police force started shooting innocent citizens. Smugglers forced to attend their own funerals BEFORE they were executed. The spurned holiday demand that ended in tragedy at the Royal High School. The real life Jekyll and Hyde and Angelical Thomas, Captain of the City Guard, hanged on Leith Walk after a lifetime of satanism.

This fascinating collection of true life crimes spans four centuries, producing a cauldron of unsavoury characters driven by greed, lust, flawed ambition and sheer recklessness.

Burke and Hare embarked on a murder spree to supply bodies for the anatomist's tables at the University but would many lives have been spared if Dr Robert Knox, their best customer, had listened to his conscience? No wonder Edinburgh bairns would chant as they played in the streets:

Up the close and doun the stair,
But and ben wi' Burke and Hare,
Burke's the butcher, Hare's the thief,
Knox the boy that buys the beef.

Some of Edinburgh's most callous murderers were brought to justice by their own bungling. Like the case of a dog whose death from arsenic poisoning trapped a wife killer. Like the schoolmaster who got deep into debt by spending too much time in the vice dens which thrived beneath the Victorian capital's thin layer of respectability. He insured his wife for £1,000, poisoned her and then tried to blame the sudden death on a gas leak.

We also learn that it was not unusual for convicted men awaiting execution to write autobiographies full of self pity. The confessions of Nicol Muschet, another wife killer, provide a particularly distasteful example of this kind of hypocrisy.

But our journey to the darker side starts in 1589 with 200 witches sailing out to sea. Their mission... to kill King James VI.

King James and the witches

IN October 1589, James VI sailed across the sea to fetch home his fifteen-year-old bride, Princess Anne of Denmark. In those days such a journey was regarded as a fairly hazardous adventure for a King. It was the only romantic gesture of James's life. But it had a sequel which was far from romantic.

Shortly after his return to Scotland, James personally presided at the "examination" of several persons who were later brought to trial for witchcraft, and particularly for plotting by sorcery to raise a storm against the King's ship.

Thus he appears in a most unpleasant role in one of Scotland's most extraordinary witchcraft cases.

According to a contemporary pamphlet entitled *Newes from Scotland*, it all began "within the towne of Trenent." There dwelt one David Seaton, "deputie bailiffe in the said town," who had a maid called Geillis Duncan.

Geillis was very active as a healer of the sick, and gave her help gladly to "all such as were troubled or grieved with anie kind of sickness or infirmitie." Eventually "the saide David Seaton had his maid in great suspicion that she did not do those things by naturall and lawful waies." He began to suspect her of witchcraft.

Incredible as it seems, the lay healing of the sick was the basis of a great many charges of sorcery. A very probable explanation is that the rising medical profession - the chirurgeon (surgeon) craft - used accusations of that kind to stamp out opposition from country herbalists and lay healers, and joined with the superstitious ministers and the others involved in sending thousands of innocent people to the torture chamber and the stake.

Once an accusation was made, and the necessary "confession" extracted by torture, nothing was too fantastic to be believed.

David Seaton asked his maid for the secret of her cures. Finding her at a loss for an answer, he and some helpers subjected her to the thumb-screws and other "grievous tortures." Thus encouraged, she revealed that her healing was done through the "wicked allurements and entisements of the Devil." Her master then dispatched her to the Tolbooth Prison.

Whether she was again tortured in the Tolbooth, or had already suffered enough at the hands of her public-spirited master, Geillis then made further confessions. She named a long list of accomplices in her dealings with the Devil, including Dr John Fian, schoolmaster at Saltpans in Lothian, and Agnes Sampson of Haddington.

The details of her confession are not recorded, but it was brought to the notice of the King, and proved of enormous interest to him. The accused were taken to Holyrood for examination before His Majesty and the Privy Council.

James was a learned man, well earning of the title of "the wisest fool in Christendom." Like most learned men of his age, because of his great wisdom and goodness, he had earned for himself the particular hatred of Satan. So he had a consuming interest in witchcraft and regarded himself an expert on it. The personal observations which he was able to make during the investigation in this case served as a basis for his erudite work on "Daemonology," with proved a great encouragement to witch-hunters.

The first witness to be examined was Agnes Sampson. She was an elderly woman with a considerable local reputation as a midwife. She stoutly denied all the charges against her. Accordingly, His Majesty ordered her to be removed to the Tolbooth to undergo torture. After suffering "payne most grevous," Agnes was ready to confess.

Her story must have exceeded King James's expectations. She said that:-

On 31st October 1589, she set out on a mission with various other witches, the total being about two hundred.

They all put out to sea, "each one in a riddle or sieve," and sailed to

North Berwick. They made merry on the voyage, drinking wine which was unaccountably available in the sieves. When they landed they joined hands and danced on the shore, singing:
    "Cummer goe ye before, cummer goe ye,
    Gif ye will not go before, cummer let me."
    Then, led by Geillis Duncan playing a reel on a "trump," they made their way to North Berwick Kirk. There Satan was waiting for them. He was in human form, but with claws on his hands and feet, "lyk the griffon." He had a nose like the beak of an eagle, and great burning eyes, and spoke in a hollow voice. He was in clerical garb, "in a blak gown, with a blak hat." Mounting the pulpit, he preached a sermon in which he picked out King James for particular abuse.
    One of the witches asked him after the sermon why he so hated James. The reply was, "By reason that the King is the greatest enemie hee hath in the world." (To James, no doubt, this gave Agnes's story the stamp of unquestionable authenticity.)
    The Devil took oaths of allegiance from all the witches at the convention. Then they put out to sea again in their sieves and returned home.
    Next, Agnes Sampson described how she and her accomplices had attempted to destroy the King by a spell which involved the use of the venom of a black toad, collected in an oyster shell. The idea, apparently, was to spill some of this on an article of the King's soiled linen. However, they failed to get access to His Majesty's laundry, so the toad's venom was wasted.
    When the King was at sea, Agnes and her colleagues went out to sea again in their sieves. They threw into the water a cat prepared for the purpose by a special Satanic ritual. This caused a storm to rise, in which a treasure ship was sunk, and the ship in which the King and his bride sailed suffered peculiarly bad weather throughout the voyage. In fact, only the saintliness of the King saved the ship from destruction.
    These revelations filled the King with a "wonderful admiration."
    The next to be examined was Dr John Fian, the only male among the accused. He, too, needed a ghastly course of treatment to induce him to confess. After suffering in the "boot," a maiming instrument of torture which inflicted "the most severe and cruell pain in the worlde," he delighted His Majesty with a long list of his sorceries.
    Of the convention in North Berwick, he told roughly the same story as Agnes Sampson. He added, however, that he was "Regester and Secretar

to the Devil," and in this office he acted as clerk to the convention.

When returned to his prison Fian announced that the Devil appeared to him in a dream, all in black and carrying a white wand, and asked for a renewal of his allegiance. Dr Fian said that he had renounced the Devil, who broke his wand in anger and then disappeared. His inquisitors regarded this as a great triumph for themselves, though there was, of course, no suggestion that it would save him from the stake. But possibly it was a ruse to disarm suspicion, for the next day the doctor managed somehow to escape.

James, in a rage, issued proclamations for his capture. He was apparently traced back to the vicinity of his school-house at Tranent, and soon he again stood, a prisoner, before the King.

To the King's horror, Dr Fian, now apparently recovered from the effects of his first ordeal, denied the charges brought against him, and repudiated the confession made under torture. To the King, this could have only one explanation.

According to the author of *Newes from Scotland*, His Majesty, "perceiving his stubborn wilfulnesse, conceived and imagined that, in the time of his absence, he had entered into a new conference and league with the Devill his maister."

Accordingly he was subjected to new and more fiendish tortures, devised by the King's ingenuity, to bring him to repentance. But somehow the doctor's nerve did not break this time, and he maintained his innocence until finally his inquisitors sent him to the stake.

When his torture was finished, he was so broken and maimed that any death, however horrible, must have seemed a sweet relief to him.

The Justiciary reports give us, in the facts set forth in the indictment, substantially the same story, but the details are somewhat different. Presumably the author of *Newes from Scotland* had his information at second or third hand.

According to Fian's indictment, he went to North Berwick Kirk by some magic conveyance which sent him skimming along the earth's surface. There he heard Satan's sermon, which is described as a sermon of "doubtsum speeches." He then went out to sea in the company of Satan—presumably in his capacity as Satan's secretary!—followed by the other witches. In this version, he went skimming over the sea "in ane boat."

The principal charge against him was that of using sorcery "For raising of wyndis att the King's passing to Denmark," and receiving the instruction from Satan: "Ye shall sink the ship." He was also charged with "assembling himself with Satan, at the King's returning from Denmark, where Satan promised to raise ane mist, and cast the King's Majestic in England." Why the Devil contented himself with aiming at driving the King into England—instead of finishing the job off properly by despatching him to the deep—the report does not make clear. "And for performing thereof," continues the indictment, "he tuik ane thing like ti ane fute-ball, quihilk apperit to the said Johnne like a wisp, and cuist the same in the sea; quihilk causit ane vapour and ane reik to ryis."

An unusual feature of the case was that the accused included two women of gentle birth, one of them a daughter of a Senator of the College of Justice. Probably there were other motives behind these charges.

One of these women, Barbara Napier, was acquitted by a majority of the jury. James himself ordered that the death sentence be pronounced, and the jurymen who had voted for her acquittal were tried for "manifest and wilful errour."

So, to the "admiration" and edification of His Majesty, the investigations and trials went on, and for a long time victims of this orgy were sent to be burned on the Castle Hill.

Apart from those who had a material interest or a spiteful motive in sending them to their deaths, and the little tyrants like Geillis Duncan's master, there were those who were no doubt sincere. Presumably the superstitious clergy firmly believed that they were wrestling with the Devil in sending his agents to the fire. Even after the repeal of the penal statutes against witchcraft in 1736, the Associate Presbytery regarded the repeal as "contrary to the express law of God."

That charges of witchcraft were taken seriously by intelligent and learned men seems incredible to a later age. Yet to our ancestors the peril to humanity through persons who had voluntarily become the Devil's agents appeared so self-evident that only fools and evil-doers could doubt it.

Murder in the High School

On the morning of September 15, 1595, Hercules Rollock, Rector of the High School of Edinburgh, arrived at the school at his usual time. He found the boys were ahead of him. They had barricaded the school doors and windows, and were ready to hold the building against all comers. Some of them appeared at an upper window and explained to the Rector that they were staying inside until the school was granted a holiday.

Hercules Rollock's heart must have sunk within him as it dawned on him that he was in for yet another "barring out" or school revolt. He would have been even more dismayed if he could have foreseen how the morning would end—in perhaps the most sensational event in the long history of the school.

At that time the school had already played its part in Edinburgh's history. It had its origins in the Abbey of Holyrood in the eleventh century. There the sons of those who had influence at Court were educated along with the future clergy. Later the lay scholars were separated from the clerical, and formed a "gramar scule" in the town. Until the Reformation the school was under the Abbot of Holyrood, who appointed the "Maister," though even before that the Town Council had been bearing the financial burden.

These holy associations make the school a strange setting for an act of homicide.

In 1519 the Town Council gave the school something of a monopoly by forbidding the citizens to "put their bairns till ony particular scule within this toun but to the principale gramar scule." Then in 1566 Queen Mary gifted the school to the Magistrates of Edinburgh, along with other Franciscan and Dominican properties. The "hie schule," as it had come to be called, was patronised by James the Sixth, who conferred on it the proud title of *Schola Regia Edimburgensis*, which it still bears.

The Royal High School is proud of its former pupils. They make an impressive and varied list, ranging from famous writers to the inventor of the telephone. However, there was one boy, Bill, who brought no credit to his school, only disgrace and trouble. Yet in the imagination of every High School boy he has a place of honour among former pupils second only to that of Sir Walter Scott himself. He was William Sinclair, the chief actor in the great "barring out" of 1595.

When William Sinclair was a pupil there, the High School was housed in a new building in the grounds of the former Blackfriars Monastery, in the place still called High School Yards. It had entered on a nourishing period under Hercules Rollock, a scholar of great distinction. But it took more than a scholar to cope with the High School boys.

At this period the boys were particularly turbulent. Several cases of "barring out" had occurred. In these days school holidays were not very long, and "barring out" was the recognised method of obtaining an extra holiday. The first step was to approach the Town Council with a request. Almost invariably it was refused. Then the boys met and chose a leader, whom they agreed to follow to the end. During the night they took possession of the school and laid in a store of provisions and lethal weapons. The masters arriving in the morning found, as Hercules Rollock did, that they and other representatives of authority were "barred out." A spokesman would appear at a window and demand a holiday. If it was refused, as it naturally would be, a state of siege commenced. Sometimes the boys held out for several days, and occasionally they won their holiday. More often the Rector appealed successfully to his patrons, the Magistrates, and the building was taken by storm.

In 1580, nine of the boys were lodged in prison after a "barring out." They were fined 40 shillings each to pay for the door which was broken in "at their taking."

Another "barring out " occurred in 1587. This time the Lord Provost himself took command of operations. The Council records describe the scene. The boys not only took it on themselves "to hald the schole agains their Maister, bot also maist proudlie and contempteously agains my Lord Provost and the bailies." The latter were therefore "compellit to ding in pieces ane of the doors." On entering they found the scholars armed "with pistols, swords, halberts, and uther weapouns and armour agains all guid order and lawes."

A fine was imposed on nine ringleaders to pay for the damage. They were also sentenced to suffer "the correctioun of their maister in the sicht of thair codisciples." We can assume that the "correctioun" was painful. It is interesting to note that one of the offenders named was "Alexr. Napier, son to the Laird of Merchestoun." The Laird of Merchiston was then the famous mathematician, John Napier, the inventor of logarithms.

As a further punishment for this "barring out," the annual school holidays were restricted to the one week from May 15 to 22, "and at na uther tymes." Any scholars even requesting an extra holiday were to suffer corporal punishment. Two years later the Council relented and allowed the boys eight days in May and eight in September.

No doubt the authorities thought that they had stamped out unruliness by this drastic treatment. For some years there was, in fact, comparative quiet. Then, in September 1595, a new storm gathered. As the autumn vacation approached, the boys became unusually restless, and bold enough to sue for an extra holiday before the vacation. On September 14 they went in a body to the Council chamber to make their request to the Magistrates. It was peremptorily refused.

Smouldering with righteous indignation, the bolder spirits among the "bairnis" prepared for action. During the night they laid in "meat, drink, pistol, and sword," and barricaded the school to withstand a siege. Thus it was that the morning of September 15 found Hercules Rollock standing in High School Yards arguing with a group of excited but determined bairns who crowded to a window above him.

For some time the learned Rector argued, threatened and cajoled. But there was no room for compromise. The Rector was determined to uphold authority, and demanded the unconditional surrender of the boys. They stood by their demand for a holiday. Neither side would give in.

Realising that arguments and threats were useless, Hercules Rollock sought the aid of the Magistrates. A force of city officers soon arrived, under the command of Baillie John McMorane.

The Baillie called on the boys to surrender. He, too, met with no success. Accordingly it was decided, as usual, to break in the door. The boys inside became more excited and defiant than ever as they saw the enemy below move a joist or beam into position for use as a battering ram. They called on the Baillie to cease operations, threatening to shoot him if he persisted.

The Baillie and his assistants did not take the threat seriously. The boys had had weapons on previous "barrings out," but they had never actually used them. McMorane's assistants set to work with a will, and the heavy beam thudded against the barred door.

At last the door showed signs of giving way under the repeated assaults. The boys became more and more apprehensive, and their threats became more violent. One scholar cried out to the Baillie to call his men off "utherwayis, he vowit to God, he would shoot ane pair of bulletis through his heid." Still the Baillie and his officers "ran with the joist to the said door."

Then, as the door seemed about to give way, William Sinclair, one of the boys' ringleaders, appeared at the window with a pistol in his hand. He leant forward and fired. Baillie McMorane fell dead to the ground, shot through the head.

A horrified silence fell on the spectators. Then the news spread like wildfire through the town. According to a contemporary diarist, "the haill tounis men ran to the schooll." The boys were too shocked to resist. Sinclair and seven others were lodged in the Tolbooth.

The Council held an extraordinary meeting to consider what to do. It was decided that the King must be informed immediately. The Lord Provost and a deputation went to break the news to His Majesty at Falkland Palace.

For King James VI, it set a most difficult and delicate problem. He did not want to offend the prosperous burgesses of Edinburgh, whose friendship he valued. Baillie McMorane had been highly respected in the city. On the other hand, the boys were the sons of noble and powerful families whom the King could even less afford to offend. William Sinclair himself was the son of the Chancellor of Caithness, and those Sinclairs were a turbulent lot who could give the King considerable trouble. Moreover, the King had a soft spot for his Schola Regia, though he can hardly have felt pleased with it now.

Of the trial of the culprits there is no existing record, but that they were tried we know from a later report. It is the report of the trial of a seventeen-year-old boy, James Middleton, who in 1612 slew his companion by stabbing him "with ane dirk, under the schorte ribis, upon the diaphragma, which is ane noble pairt." The defence took objection to the indictment on the ground of the accused's youth. The case of the Chancellor of Caithness's son and the rest of the bairnes for "John McMorane's slauchter" was quoted as an authority. The Crown pointed out that, though the boys in the McMorane case were acquitted, they were all under fourteen years of age, and that the decision was reached "by His Majesty's expres warrand." So the King apparently intervened to have the boys released.

Another interesting sidelight on the case is provided by a petition presented to the King and the Privy Council by the seven boys arrested with Sinclair. They all stoutly contend that they are innocent and "are willing to abyde tryale befoir ane unsuspect (impartial) Juge." Their complaint was that the Provost and Baillies, to whom commission to try them had been

given, "were partiall, they being in effect baith juge and pairty." They further complain that when they were brought before this prejudiced tribunal, their legal defence proved unassailable. Their "juges, seeing that they could not get their intent, and mynding na thing else bot to wearie and rack thame with expenssis," continued the case till a further day. Then they again continued it till a further day, so that it seemed likely to go on indefinitely till the boys would be wearied into pleading guilty.

The petitioners craved the privilege of a jury drawn from outside Edinburgh, but the influence of the King would probably have saved those aristocratic little ruffians in any case.

The only sufferers as a result of the incident—apart from John McMorane's family—were the Rector, Hercules Rollock, who was dismissed; the masters, whose salaries were cut; and the school itself, which suffered a great loss of prestige, as well as of pupils. Parents were naturally afraid to send their boys to the school for some time after the murder.

That was the last of the "barrings out." The High School boys did not, however, become angels. They figure in the famous "bickers" with the College (University) lads, which went on to a later period. The most noted of these was, of course, the occasion when, led by the Earl of Haddington, Lord President of the Court of Session and himself an old High School boy, they chased the College lads along the Cowgate, through the Grassmarket and out of the West Port. His Lordship then had the gate shut on the enemy, causing them to spend the night in the fields.

But no more is heard of High School boys carrying lethal weapons. Nevertheless, Rule XVII of the School Regulations still reads: "No gunpowder, fireworks, or firearms of any description are permitted to be brought within the grounds, under penalty of confiscation, and such punishment as may be necessary." The rule is still read out annually to an assembly of bairns, among whom sit potential Walter Scotts, but—presumably—no potential slayers of magistrates.

The Laird of Warriston

Warriston Road and Warriston Crescent bear the name of the old estate of Warriston, the scene of one of the most sensational crimes of its day. In that age events which made a great impression on people's minds became the subjects of popular ballads. The ballads of the death of the Laird of Warriston keep alive the memory of this crime.

On June 26, 1604, Robert Weir, sometime servant of the Laird of Dunipace, was tried and sentenced to be broken on the Wheel for his part in the murder of John Kincaid, the Laird of Warriston. Four years before that, Jean Livingston, the young and beautiful Lady Warriston (as the Laird's wife was called by courtesy), a daughter of the Laird of Dunipace, had been tried and put to death, along with her nurse and a serving woman, for the same crime.

We have no record of their trial. What we know we learn from the brief report of Weir's trial, and from the extraordinary account of the Lady of Warriston's conversion and repentance. The latter was recorded by the minister who attended to her spiritual needs in her last hours.

In June, 1600, Lady Warriston sent a serving woman to fetch Robert Weir from the Abbey of Holyrood, where the Laird of Dunipace was in attendance on the King. He came to her at Warriston, but that day "he could get no speech from her." Perhaps her nerve had failed her.

But on July 1 she sent her nurse to summon Weir again. This time she had regained her nerve, and told Weir why she had sent for him. She had conceived a deadly rancour, hatred, and malice against her husband. She had decided that he must be killed. Weir agreed to do the killing.

Lady Warriston then conveyed him to a low cellar in the house of Warriston. He stayed hidden there until midnight, when she came and fetched him. She led him up through the hall of the darkened house, and into the room where the Laird was sleeping.

When they went in Weir rushed at the sleeping man, and struck him. The Laird woke and struggled violently for his life. He fell out of bed, and the two men struggled on the floor. The Laird shouted for help, and cried out with pain, as Weir began to strangle him. The sight was too much for Lady Warriston. Leaping wildly over the bed, she rushed out of the room into the hall. There she sat, pressing her hands to her ears to shut out her husband's cries. At last Weir came out to her and told her that the Laird was dead.

Perhaps it was only then that the full meaning of what she had done became clear to her. The murder had been crudely brutal, and almost unconcealed. The servants must have heard the Laird's cries. Besides, what she had seen and heard had no doubt wakened her out of the trance of hatred which up to then had obscured the horror of her crime.

Panic-stricken, she begged Weir to take her away with him. For, as she later said, "I feared tryall." But Weir told her to stay. "If this matter comes not to light," he said, "you shall say he died in the gallery, and I shall return to my master's service. But if it be known, I shall fly and take the crime on me, and none dare pursue you."

Lady Warriston agreed to stay. She cannot have hoped that the crime would remain undetected. But her father was a courtier, close to the King. "Flesh and blood" made her think that his influence would save her.

We can only guess what had led Lady Warriston to take the terrible decision to murder her husband. She alleged that he had bitten her in the arm and had struck her several times. There is no particular reason to doubt that, but it can only have been the immediate provocation.

Perhaps she had been married to a much older man, whom she hated and rebelled against. Certainly the Warriston and Dunipace families had property and influence. Her marriage to Warriston must have been a "good marriage" in the eyes of her family, a union of two important houses.

The Laird himself may have been bad-tempered and even brutal. So his alleged assaults would suggest. It may be that an old and rejected husband jealously accused her of unfaithfulness. She had a recently-born child at the time of the murder, and one ballad writer makes the Laird deny that the child is his. Perhaps she had a lover. It may be that she was cold-bloodedly cruel.

But the way that the murder was committed does not suggest a cunning, scheming murderess. And whatever the cause of her hatred, it was shared by her nurse—the "false nourice" of the ballad writers. For when her Lady sent her to Holyrood for Weir, the nurse knew what he was wanted for. She went willingly, and said that if she did not find him, "she would do it herself." That can hardly be explained merely by loyalty to her Lady.

We can only guess, too, why Robert Weir agreed to murder, and to risk a horrible death for himself in consequence, and why Lady Warriston confided in him and relied on him. The fact that she asked him to take her away with him and his willingness to take the blame on himself suggest he was no hired assassin.

Can there have been love between him and Lady Warriston, on whom he must so often have attended when she was a young girl on her father's estate in Stirling or about the King's Court? Had her marriage separated them and left him with a hatred of the man he was to murder?

Or had Lady Warriston enjoyed the humble and worshipping devotion from afar of this unfortunate youth? And had she cynically exploited his devotion to lead him into murder? It is tempting to speculate.

The crime was discovered immediately. No doubt servants who had heard the cries, and saw the Laird's body on the following morning, took the news to Edinburgh. Officers of justice came to Warriston. Lady Warriston tried to put on a show of grief, but no tears would come.

Certainly this shows her still, as it did then, in a bad light.

She was arrested, along with her nurse and two serving women, and taken to the Tolbooth. They were tried before the Magistrates of Edinburgh, who then had power to try murderers caught red-handed.

Lady Warriston, the nurse and one of the serving women were condemned to be burnt at the stake after being strangled. Possibly evidence was obtained, by torture or other persuasion, from the other serving woman. Weir fled and was a fugitive from justice for four years.

The serving woman who was condemned to death was probably an innocent victim of the crime. Her offence seems to have been that, when the crime was committed, out of loyalty or fear she did not tell what she knew.

Lady Warriston's confidence that her family would help her was unfounded. They turned against her because she had brought dishonour to their name. Their influence at Court was directed to having her put to death as quickly and quietly as possible, to avoid undesirable publicity. The only advantage gained by her exalted rank was that the method of her execution was altered to a less horrible one. She was beheaded.

None of her family came to comfort her in her last hours. Only her murdered husband's brother kissed her and forgave her before her death. The nurse and the poor serving woman died at the stake, being of less exalted rank. All three died at 3 o'clock on the morning of July 5. This time was chosen under pressure from her relatives, who thought that there would be fewer spectators then.

In the brief time between her trial and her death Lady Warriston underwent her strange conversion and repentance, under the guidance of a minister who was in constant attendance on her. Before her trial she had rejected his ministrations, but after her conviction a remarkable change came over her.

Before her trial she had apparently hoped to escape death; after it she prepared to face death. The minister was so pleased with her conversion that he remained with her practically all the time, allowing her only a few hours of sleep.

He called in one of his brethren to witness this miracle. The news spread, and people crowded to the door of the prison and collected in the streets outside.

Lady Warriston professed true repentance for her crime, and began to look forward eagerly to her death. She prayed with the minister and discoursed with him endlessly on spiritual things. It seemed to him that he was listening to the words of a saint, and he began to keep a record of what she said.

However much of her state of mind was produced by sincere religious experience, and however much by delirium, it enabled her to meet her death with complete calm. The minister at one stage turned his attentions to the nurse, but without success. He does not appear to have concerned himself with the serving woman.

Four years later Robert Weir paid for his crime according to his sentence. Terrible though the crime was, we cannot to-day avoid a feeling of horror at the thought of the revolting forms of execution by which the murderers—and one practically innocent woman, in all likelihood—were punished. It is difficult to imagine that our ancestors accepted them as a matter of course.

Major Weir

To our ancestors, the Devil was a very real and active participant in their affairs. They believed that in various human forms, or as a bird or beast, or in his own true form with forked tail and cloven hoof, he travelled the towns and villages of Scotland, and gave supernatural powers to those who became his agents. Against those suspected of being his agents, Church and secular power waged a merciless campaign.

For many years this was a dark and terrible thing. After 1597, when the General Assembly of the Kirk threatened to excommunicate any Magistrate who did not sentence witches to death, the great witch-hunt was on. Thousands of victims, mostly women of the poorer classes, suffered terrible deaths for witchcraft. Their convictions sometimes followed on voluntary confessions, produced by insane delusions, but were generally induced by the most revolting tortures. Not until 1722 was the last "witch" burnt in Sutherland. In 1736 the penal statutes against witchcraft were repealed.

The case of Major Weir and his sister was not a typical witchcraft case. They were not, in fact, put to death for witchcraft. But they were long remembered in Edinburgh tradition as sinners who had made a compact with the Devil.

Thomas Weir was born in Carluke in 1599. He served as an officer under Leslie in Ireland, and in the Covenanting army against Montrose in 1644-45, rising to the rank of major.

On his retirement from active service, he became a captain of Edinburgh City Guard. In this office he is said to have commanded the guard at the execution of Montrose in 1650. Shortly afterwards he retired, and devoted himself, ostensibly, to religion.

Major Weir's religion was that of the strictest Covenanting sect. Accordingly, he soon moved from his lodgings in the Cowgate to take up house with his sister in the West Bow, where that sect had its stronghold.

The West Bow, of which little remains now, was a street of tall lands, making a zig-zag descent from the Lawnmarket on the south side of the ridge of the Old Town. At the foot it led into the Grassmarket, the old place of execution, where, in their day, Covenanting heroes laid down their lives for the faith, "and bade eloquent farewell to sun, moon and stars, and earthly friendships, or died silent to the roll of drums."

As the martyrs of the Covenant were its glory, the sect of the West

Bow represented its discredit. They were the stiffnecked burgesses and "divines" who considered themselves the "elect." They made a great show of piety and godliness and excelled all others at prayer. In an age when people were fined, or even whipped, for breaking the Sabbath, and patrols searched the streets during divine service to seize anyone walking abroad, they were the most holy of the holy. Their enemies nicknamed them the "Bowhead Saints."

In the "sanctified bends" of the West Bow, Major Weir was in his element. With his military record, and his former office in the City Guard, he enjoyed great prestige among the "Saints." It was their custom to meet in each other's houses to pray, and among them Major Weir "prayed to admiration."

A tall black man, with a "grim countenance and a big nose," and usually clad in a dark cloak, he must have made an imposing figure. Standing among the brethren, leaning on a tall staff carved with centaurs' heads, which he was never without, he prayed in a "ravishing accent" marked by a graceful whining and sighing, which made him the envy of the ministers. He could quote Scripture at length and most effectively. People came from miles around to hear him pray, and some thought him more angel than man. Among the enraptured ladies of the Bowhead, he was known as "Angelical Thomas."

Not that he would pray in any house indiscriminately! He would only pray in the houses of those who were "Saints of the highest Form." Thus the most respectable families competed to entice the Major to their homes. If successful, they would pack in as many guests as they could, for his presence there was proof that they were numbered among the "elect."

So the years passed, and the Major became the unofficial leader of the "Saints." He was greatly in demand as a spiritual adviser, and was employed by many persons to solve the scruples of their consciences. To the wives of his flock, he was a specially valued guide. His reputation for inspired piety spread far and wide.

Then, one spring day in 1670, when he was in his seventieth year, Major Weir cast aside his cloak of holiness. There was a large and distinguished gathering of the "elect " in his audience chamber. The newcomers, awed at finding themselves in the inner temple of the Bowhead, were curious to hear the great man pray. Then the moment came. Major Weir, venerable and saintly, rose amongst them, leaning on his staff. A reverent hush fell on the gathering.

But it was not prayer that they heard. For a few seconds their minds must have refused to admit what fell upon their ears. Sparing them no details, he began to tell them of the sinful life he'd led. "Angelical Thomas" was only a facade, behind which the real Major Weir had committed every carnal offence. His life had not been merely dissipated, but utterly depraved.

It would have been easy enough to shock that assembly in the West Bow, but the Major's crimes would have shocked all but the most depraved in any society in any century. Men to whose families he had been spiritual adviser must have looked apprehensively at their wives. What the ladies felt as his indecent reminiscences fell on their delicate ears, we can only guess.

"Before God," he said, "I have not told you the hundred part of what I can say more, and am guilty of!"

When they collected their senses, the congregation, with consternation written on every face, rose from their places, and we can imagine the anguished discussions of what they should do. Their hastily arrived at decision was that the whole thing must be hushed up. Major Weir was the very flower of their sect, and his revelations would deal a terrible blow to them. In all likelihood they probably suspected, and with good reason, that he was insane.

The Major, who was by now frail, was bundled off to his room and kept a virtual prisoner there. The news was given out that he was gravely ill.

For some months they thus protected his reputation and that of the "Saints." But there had been in the congregation who witnessed his self-exposure the Rev. John Sinclair, Minister of Ormiston. He felt a certain professional jealousy of "Angelical Thomas." After some long hesitation he reported the affair to Sir Andrew Ramsay, the Lord Provost.

The Lord Provost could not believe it. He could only conclude it was a case of mental disorder. He sent some eminent physicians to examine the Major. Their report was that he was sound in body and mind, and suffering only from an "exulcerated conscience." His one desire was that he should be brought to justice. Some eminent clergymen were then sent to him and confirmed the physicians' opinion.

Accordingly, the Town Guard arrested their old captain and also his sister, Jean, whom his confessions had implicated. As they were arrested, Jean warned the Guard to keep his staff away from him, as it would give him magical powers over them. They accepted her advice, and took the staff into custody.

In the Tolbooth, Jean explained at greater length that the staff was a magic symbol given to her brother by the Devil. It gave him the power to commit all manner of sins with impunity, to pray divincly, and, curiously enough in view of his record, the power to reconcile estranged husbands and wives! All this the Major confirmed.

The prisoners were visited by all the great clergy of Scotland, for whom Major Weir willingly expanded on his former confession. But he firmly refused to repent, and any offer to pray for him met with refusal.

Jean was equally communicative, but her revelations mostly concerned her dealings with the Devil. She put back her head-dress and frowned, and the horrified clergy saw on her wrinkled forehead the Devil's mark in the shape of a horse-shoe. She told them how, on September 7, 1648, she and her brother were transported from Edinburgh to Musselburgh in a coach which seemed all afire. There they met the Devil and made a compact with him.

The Weirs were tried in the Justiciary Court at Edinburgh on April 9, 1670. The Major was charged mainly with carnal offences. Jean faced similar charges, but the main charges against her were of sorcery.

The indictment set forth that she committed sorceries when "she lived and keeped a school at Dalkeith, when she took employment from a woman to speak on her behalf to the Queen of ffairie, meaning the Devil." The Devill also gave her a piece of tree or root and told her that it would enable her to do as she pleased. On another occasion the Devil, in the form of a woman, instructed her to stand with her hands on the crown of her head and repeat thrice the words, "All my crosses and troubles go alongst to the doors," which the indictment solemnly declared to be "truly a consulting with the Devil and Act of Sorcery, these things being done by none but Devils and Sorcerers and such as correspond with them."

Proof was led in Major Weir's case, since the King's Advocate did not think his plea of guilty was emphatic enough. But for this we would be tempted to think that his earthly offences were as imaginary as his association with the Devil. Jean's plea of guilty was accepted.

The court found them guilty of the earthly offences charged, but decided to disregard the charges of sorcery as too vague. This alone sets the trial aside from most other witchcraft trials, where the hope of acquittal was almost non-existent.

Major Weir suffered a horrible death at the stake on the Gallow Lee, an old place of execution between Edinburgh and Leith, near the site now occupied by the Playhouse Theatre. Asked for the last time to pray, he

said:—"Let me alone. I have lived as a beast, and I must die as a beast." It was widely believed that, having offended his Heavenly Master, he was anxious not to offend the Devil.

Jean Weir was hanged in the Grassmarket. Her behaviour at the end confirmed that she was completely insane. Whether the Major was insane by the standards of modern Courts is an interesting speculation.

Long after the horror of witchcraft trials and burning at the stake had been forgotten, and Burns had reduced the Devil to a figure of fun, the Weirs remained a persistent Edinburgh legend. The house known as "Major Weir's Land" was dreaded by citizens who had to make their way past it at night, and no occupant could be found for it.

In the very midst of the "Bowhead Saints," the Devil had established an outpost which none dared invade. It was said that the Weirs returned there by night to revel with other damned spirits, and late passers-by would see the broken windows lighted up, and forms flitting past as they danced to ghostly music. The magic staff, it was rumoured, returned to perform its former duties, including that of opening the door to the visitors from Hell.

Sometimes late revellers returning from the taverns would have to dash wildly to the side of the road for safety as Major Weir went galloping past them on a headless charger in a rush of flame. And Robert Louis Stevenson's father handed down to him the tradition that sometimes there would be heard the rattle of wheels and the clatter of hooves on the cobblestones, and " the Devil's coach, drawn by six coal-black horses, with fiery eyes, would drive at night into the West Bow, and belated people might see the dead Major through the glass."

About 1820, a prospective tenant, a dissolute soldier named William Patullo, decided to brave the haunted house which had stood vacant for a century and a half. On the first night, when he and his wife were settling down to sleep, a beast "somewhat like a calf" rose from the bottom of the bed and stared down at them for a while. Then it vanished. Next morning the terrified Patullos vanished too, and the house stood vacant again till 1878. In that year it was demolished with most of the street.

So there is no longer any chance that belated revellers may suddenly see a coach "all aflame," drawn by six coal-black horses with fiery eyes, go thundering into the West Bow, and Major Weir—or even His Satanic Majesty, "the Muckle Deil himsel"—alight to join the revels in the haunted Land.

A case of piracy

In the autumn of 1704, the English ship *Worcester* sailed into the Forth and cast anchor off Burntisland. Her master, Captain Thomas Green, intended to refit after meeting bad weather at sea. He cannot have guessed the interest his arrival created. But to many people in Edinburgh the *Worcester's* arrival was like the answer to a prayer for vengeance.

Scotland was smarting under the humiliation of the Darien fiasco. Six years earlier, a small fleet of Scottish ships had sailed from Leith to found the Colony of Caledonia on the Isthmus of Darien. This was the climax of an ambitious scheme hatched in the mind of William Paterson, chiefly remembered as the founder of the Bank of England.

Paterson was one of many Scotsmen who believed that Scotland could share in the expanding commercial prosperity of England. A "Company of Scotland trading to Africa and the Indies"—the ill-fated Darien Company—was established by an Act of the Scots Parliament. Its main purpose anticipated the idea of the Panama Canal.

The Darien Colony would establish a trade route linking the Atlantic and the Pacific. Scotland would grow prosperous from the immense trade which would flow through this route. Subscription lists were opened in Edinburgh and London, and the capital was quickly subscribed.

The East India Company in England was alarmed, and the English Parliament petitioned the King. Scotland, it was claimed, would become a free port for East India commodities and could undersell England in foreign markets. The King made known his hostility to the scheme and his displeasure with the Scots. A Bill was introduced imposing severe penalties on any Englishmen who subscribed to or assisted in the Darien scheme. English investors hastily withdrew their subscriptions.

The scheme was thus doomed from the start. It could never have succeeded in the face of English and Royal determination to kill it. But Scotland's pride was aroused. Scotsmen subscribed as a matter of patriotism, and the English subscriptions were soon made up. A great crowd gathered at Leith to see the colonists set out.

The scheme was a calamitous failure. The causes were many — inadequate resources, mismanagement, disease and attacks by the Spaniards, who claimed the territory.

The Spanish attacks were encouraged by the English Government and the King. Worst of all, in May 1699, when the colony was on its last legs, proclamations were issued in the King's name by the Governors of the English Atlantic Colonies. They forbade the King's subjects, on pain of the severest punishment, to have any correspondence with or give any assistance to the Scottish colonists, "by arms, ammunition, provisions, or anything whatsoever."

Reinforcements sent out from Scotland found the colony deserted. Of nine Scottish ships, only one returned to Scotland. A third detachment of reinforcements found the Spanish in occupation.

The Scots naturally put all the blame on England - and the King. Feelings of resentment and wounded pride reached boiling point. By this time Queen Anne was on the throne. The Act of Security, withholding recognition of the English monarch as monarch of Scotland until Scots interests were secured, was passed by the Scots Parliament in 1704.

The final affront was not directly connected with the Darien Colony. The Darien ship, the *Annandale*, fitted out for the East Indies trade, was seized in the Downs by the East India Company, and forfeited to them by the English Courts.

Even at this distance in time from the event, we can easily imagine our ancestors' angry resentment. It was into the middle of this situation that the *Worcester* sailed, to tempt fate and the Scots.

Those most interested in vengeance were naturally the officials of the Darien Company. The authorities took no steps to stop them. So the Company's secretary, a Mr Mackenzie, hit on a daring plan. On August 12, 1704, he set out for Leith with eleven bold followers, well supplied with weapons and plenty of brandy.

They went aboard the *Worcester* like a party of jovial citizens on a Saturday outing. They were no doubt particularly welcomed for their large supply of brandy, with which they liberally treated the officers and men. Soon they were all having an excellent party.

At the height of the merry-making the twelve Scotsmen overpowered and disarmed the English crew of thirty-six men and put them ashore. They then seized the *Worcester* in the name of the Darien Company. Next day a prize crew took over the ship and laid her up securely in Burntisland Harbour.

Proceedings were instituted before the High Court of Admiralty, who were in effect invited to deal with the *Worcester* as the English Courts had dealt with the *Annandale*. Unfortunately, that was only the beginning. One of the Darien ships fitted for the East Indies trade was named *Speedy Return*, though, like most of the others, she never returned. Captain Drummond, one of the company's best officers, had sailed on her. Rumours had reached Scotland that she had been taken by pirates and her crew murdered. Gradually the *Worcester's* crew fell under suspicion.

Which came first, the suspicion or the grounds for suspicion, it would be hard to say. Some unguarded statements of the crew hinted at dark and terrible deeds done at sea. A night or two after the seizure of the *Worcester*, George Haines, one of her crew, was making merry at Leith with some Scots. He appears to have taken his enforced stay in Scotland philosophically.

The talk turned to the exploits of privateers. Haines, expansive with liquor, boasted, "Lord God, our sloop was more terrible upon the coast of Malabar." Scottish ears pricked up. Asked if he knew of the Scottish ships which had sailed to these parts, he admitted, after some persuasion, that he did.

Asked what exactly he knew, he said, " It's no great matter —you need not trouble your head about 'em, for I believe you won't see 'em in haste." Pressed for an explanation, he avoided answering, then declared, "They had turned pirrats."

Later Haines fell in with a pretty young lady called Anne Seton. Foolishly, he gave her the secrets of his heart. They did not long remain secrets. (Is it uncharitable to wonder if Anne Seton had a connection with the Darien Company?) Soon the *Speedy Return* and the *Worcester* were linked in the excited gossip of the town.

On January 2, 1705, the Privy Council ordered the examination of the *Worcester's* cargo. Proceedings were instituted against Captain Green and his crew for piracy and murder. Four of the crew were admitted as Queen's evidence.

The charge was that the accused did, "Upon one or other of the days of February, March, April or May, in the year 1703, encounter or meet with another ship or vessel, manned by its own crew upon the coast of Malabar, near Calicute—the said vessel bearing a red flag, and having English or Scotch aboard, at least such as spoke the English language," and that they attacked and captured her, killed her crew, seized her cargo and then sold the ship.

The *Speedy Return* was not mentioned, and the victims were

unidentified. In fact, the prosecution could not point to any specific act of piracy. But the conclusion the jury in the High Court of Admiralty was invited to draw was obvious.

There was a long debate on the technical objections to the indictment, all of which were repelled. Then evidence was led before a jury, the first witness being a black cook's mate. An unsuccessful attempt was made to exclude his evidence on the ground that he was a heathen. He had been on board the Worcester when she attacked and captured a ship bearing English colours between Tellicherry and Calicut. The crew were murdered with hatchets. The cargo was taken on board and the ship was sold at Callicoiloan. The first mate told him he would be thrown overboard if he said anything about it to anyone.

A black servant of Captain Green's, who for some reason had been chained and nailed to the floor of the forecastle at the time had heard the firing. The cook's mate had come and related the incident to him—including the first mate's threat.

The ship's surgeon, who was ashore at the time, had heard the firing out at sea. Next morning, he saw the *Worcester* about five miles off shore, with another ship riding at her stern. When he went on board he saw the decks lumbered with chests and bales. He was called on to dress the wounds of the crew but found them reticent about how they had come by them.

Two Leith shipmasters, who had examined the Worcester's cargo by order of the Privy Council, gave evidence that the goods were neither numbered nor marked in the usual way. Another witness told how, before the seizure of the *Worcester* the first mate had shown him a Darien Company seal which he possessed.

Anne Seton and others gave evidence of Haines's indiscreet statements. On one occasion, for example, he had said: "It is a wonder that, since we did not sink at sea, God does not make the ground open and swallow us up when we are come ashore, for the wickedness that has been committed this last voyage on board of that old bitch"—pointing to the *Worcester*. He was obviously a man suffering the pangs of conscience!

Captain Green's journals were produced. They included instructions from his owners to communicate with them in cypher through a third party. Certainly he had not been engaged in normal trading.

On that evidence, all the accused, except one who had been ashore at the relevant time, were sentenced to death.

The sensation and indignation caused in England by the convictions were immense. The Queen demanded a reprieve pending an inquiry. This, unfortunately for justice, made the carrying out of the sentences a matter of national pride. On April 11, the unfortunate Privy Council met to consider a reprieve, fully aware that the Queen urgently desired one.

The Privy Council were more impressed by the great crowd which gathered outside Parliament Hall, loudly demanding there should be no reprieve. The Council, in fact, had no choice. They were more afraid of the crowd outside than they were of the Queen. They decided against a reprieve and the news was greeted with great popular approval.

But, when the Chancellor was leaving in his coach the rumour got round that the crowd had been deceived. They set on his coach and wrecked it, while he ran for the nearest shelter. Our ancestors were no respecters of persons.

Captain Green, his first mate and his gunner were hanged on Leith Sands. The other executions were never carried out.

This was the sorry end of a tragic story. It brought the two countries to the brink of war, and, in a way, hastened the Union. Vengeance, and not justice, was satisfied, and Scotland can take no pride in the trial of Captain Green and his crew.

Yet, even without looking at the confessions made after their conviction by Haines and another member of the crew, we can be fairly sure of one thing; Captain Green and his men were obviously guilty of piracy and murder. We cannot feel they were innocent men.

If the Scots sense of justice was deranged for a time, it was perhaps not unnatural. The Scots had learned a hard lesson. They had tried to compete with England in a game where there were few rules and only the strongest survived. Perhaps they had not realised how few the rules were.

Nicol Muschet of Boghall

Where one enters the Queen's Park from Meadowbank, a low cairn stands by the side of the Duke's Walk opposite the East Lodge. Probably few passers-by know that it marks the approximate spot of a notorious crime. There, on October 17, 1720, after a long course of persecution and of attempts on her life, Nicol Muschet took his wife and murdered her "with uncommon barbarity." For that crime he was sentenced to death in the High Court of Justiciary on December 5, 1720.

It would have been no great loss to the world if Nicol Muschet had been forgotten. But men may be remembered for the evil they do as well as for the good. The crime so shocked Muschet's contemporaries that, "in testimony of abhorrence," they erected a cairn on the spot. The cairn was removed in the early years of the nineteenth century when the footpath was widened.

With the removal of this visible memorial of his crime, Muschet might at last have been forgotten. But a few years later he found a more permanent memorial in the pages of Sir Walter Scott. For, in *The Heart of Midlothian*, when Jeanie Deans meets her sister's lover in the Queen's Park by night, the meeting place is by Nicol Muschet's cairn. Scott used the horrible associations of the place to create an atmosphere of eeriness and superstitious dread, and the evil spirit of Nicol Muschet pervades the scene. So, as long as Scott's masterpiece is read, people will be curious to know something of Nicol Muschet's career.

That such curiosity can be satisfied is due largely to the information given in the *Last Speech and Confession of Nicol Muschet of Boghal*, which appeared after his death. It gave a full account of the circumstances of the crime for which he had been punished, together with "Reflections upon the preceding passages of his life, declaring his Sense of Sin." It was printed and sold by "John Reid, in Pearson's Close, a little above the Cross."

Like all such confessions, it sold well. A new edition appeared later, with the description, "Being one of the greatest and most penitent Speeches ever Published." The last edition was brought out in 1818 by Oliver and Boyd, who advertised it as "fraught with instruction to all classes, but more particularly to the young, to shun the very appearance of evil."

It actually goes a little beyond what most readers would require in the way of moral instruction.

The confessions of condemned criminals which appeared regularly in the past nearly all fall into the same pattern. They begin and end with the statement of a high moral purpose—to atone for a life of crime by putting others on their guard. The lesson always is that crime does not pay. In many cases they were probably written by prison chaplains, whose influence can nearly always be traced.

In the days when fathers took their children to see public executions as a practical lesson in the wisdom of following the paths of virtue, these confessions were probably treated seriously as part of the moral instruction of the young. Besides, it would be uncharitable to discount their sincerity in most cases.

Muschet's *Confession* follows the usual pattern, but his sincerity seems more than usually open to doubt. Written in a canting and hypocritical style, it is directed particularly to the young. He declares his purpose to be to "leave an ample testimony against the many gross and enormous transgressions I have been guilty of since my infancy—that all youth may be aware of themselves, by my example, lest by their going on in such wicked courses of life as I have done, they provoke a holy and just God to abandon and suffer them to fall into some great sins."

Like many sterner moralists, Muschet apparently believed that young people are naturally inclined to wickedness and crime unless checked by terrible threats and examples.

Throughout the pamphlet, however, his chief aim seems to be to exculpate himself by blackening the character of his unfortunate wife. It is this which makes Muschet's memory even less fragrant than it would otherwise have been.

Nicol Muschet had "the blessing to be descended of godly parents." They were anxious to discharge their duty to Nicol, who was apparently their favourite child. He was, however, an obstinate and rebellious son, notwithstanding "the many good admonitions and reproofs." While his father was alive, he willingly received his parents' instruction. After his father's death he became the Laird of Boghall. His mother continued to discharge her duties conscientiously, and was "very diligent to cause me to haunt the company of the godly."

For some time all went well. Then the young laird began to rebel against the restrictions of home life. He began to forsake godliness, partly because of natural weakness of character, and partly—as he cynically but not altogether unjustly put it—"not to appear any way singular in the world." He found it a burden to his spirit to be under subjection to his mother. In order to pursue his own course unhampered by his mother and family friends, he decided to become a medical student at Edinburgh.

In Edinburgh, young Nicol fell in with bad company. Edinburgh in those days seems to have been a particularly wicked city. As it is put in an "elegy" which was published along with his Confession,

"To fair Edina came the country lad
Where he drops all the piety he had."

In all fairness to Edinburgh, it seems, on his own confession, that he came with very little piety to drop.

High in his list of evil practices he places "walking, talking, idle discourse, reading plays, romances, or the like on the Sabbath Day." It was probably due to the influence of the clergy in these confessions that criminal careers were nearly always traced back to breaking the Sabbath Day.

In 1716, on completing his training, he became an apprentice to a surgeon at Alloa. After some time, it seems, his master's practice became rather poor, so Nicol returned home. He apparently decided to live the life of a country laird. Soon, however, he saw an advertisement of a dissection in Edinburgh. In those days dissections were comparatively rare and were events of particular professional interest. Nicol Muschet came back to Edinburgh to see it, and decided to stay.

He became an assistant in an apothecary's shop, which was then quite a normal course for a young medical practitioner. His mother continued to keep an eye on him, visiting him frequently in Edinburgh. This good woman's exhortations, however, had no effect on her son, who regarded her advice as a great "weariness." Nevertheless, he records that in this period he behaved himself comparatively well.

The period came to an end with what he regarded as the crowning tragedy of his life. That was his marriage, which he refers to as "that unlucky marriage, whereto I was led as an ox to the slaughter, and as a fool to the correction of the stocks." In 1719 he met Margaret, the daughter of Adam Hall, a merchant on the Castle Hill. According to his account, she chased him relentlessly, while he was the innocent prey of a scheming and wicked woman. Certainly it appears that she fell in love with him at once, and never lost her affection for him in spite of his brutal treatment of her. However that may be, he claimed to have been under constant pressure from her friends to marry her, and "they so far prevailed upon my simple easy temper, as to propose the matter to her father."

Margaret's father opposed the match. But, after a period of what he represents as manoeuvring on her part, they were married on September 5, 1719. Later he was bitterly to regret having courted "a person of whose piety and virtue I had so few proofs." Moreover, he could not forgive himself for having contracted his marriage according to "the sinful superstitions of the Church of England, contrary to my baptismal and national vows and my conscience," by a form "contrary to the order and decency which Christ has appointed in his Church, and the good laws of men have established." It is interesting to speculate on whether these scruples show the influence of the prison chaplain who assisted in writing the confession. Otherwise we must conclude that, whatever else he became, Nicol Muschet remained a sound Presbyterian to the end.

After two months of marriage, Muschet had decided to go abroad and desert his wife. This design was delayed by the arrangements for the administration of his estate in his absence. The arrangements were complicated by his desire so to arrange matters that his wife would be deprived of any financial support from the estate. Another complication arose in the form of James Campbell of Burnbank, a former laird who had wasted his inheritance and was now an ordnance storekeeper at the Castle. Burnbank had a claim of some kind on the Muschet estate, and the negotiations over it led to a friendship between himself and Muschet.

Burnbank is described in the confession as "the only Vice-regent of the Devil." Certainly he prompted Muschet to take the course which led him to the gallows. He advised him that he could get rid of his wife by a fraudulent divorce action, and agreed to arrange this for a consideration of £50. A complicated plot was laid to entice Margaret to a house where an agent of Burnbank's would arrange for her to be found in an apparently compromising situation. The scheme was carried out, at considerable expense, only for the conspirators to find that there was not enough evidence to satisfy the law. At Burnbank's instigation, Muschet decided to murder his wife.

The first method tried was death by poisoning. Muschet gave his wife a quantity of mercury mixed with sugar, which he administered in a dram. She became violently ill, but did not die. It was tried again, but still failed. After keeping the poor woman in agony for a long period, the plan was abandoned. Shortly afterwards, Muschet fell out with Burnbank.

The next plan tried was the simple one of arranging for accomplices to attack Margaret and murder her in a close. This was tried several times, but, by sheer good luck, Margaret escaped each time. She did not turn up at

the place where the assassin waited, or for some other reason the plot failed. It seems possible, in fact, that the accomplices, who were well paid for their services, deliberately bungled the plots so that they could extort more money out of Muschet.

Month after month the fantastic series of murderous plots continued. Finally, in October 1720, Muschet decided to do the deed himself.

On October 17, after dark, he asked his wife to come out with him. He said they were going to Duddingston, though he apparently did not explain why. Margaret, whose affection and loyalty to her husband remained absolute till the end, went with him. They went into the Queen's Park, and made their way past the Palace into the Duke's Walk. Margaret said that this was not the way to Duddingston. She seemed to sense the danger. As Muschet described it, " She weep'd and prayed that God might forgive me if I was taking her to any mischief." Apparently her tears had no effect on him. At the east end of the Walk, he turned on her and murdered her. Then he fled from the spot.

Next morning the body was discovered. Beside it was found a man's Holland sleeve, with the letter "N" sewn on it. For several days Muschet evaded detection. But some of his accomplices, no doubt thinking that he would be discovered sooner or later, and anxious to safeguard their own position, gave information to the authorities. Nicol Muschet was arrested and brought to trial.

At the trial, he offered no defence. Brought before a jury, he pleaded guilty and was sentenced accordingly.

After the publication of *The Heart of Midlothian*, a new cairn was erected to mark the scene of the murder. It could not be erected on the original spot; nor was it erected at the place, below the ruins of St. Anthony's chapel, where, for the purposes of his story, Scott depicted the old cairn. But it was placed as near as possible to the original spot.

Thus, by a curious accident, Nicol Muschet is remembered among the famous criminals of Edinburgh history. Among these he ranks with the most infamous.

The Porteous riots

In its day the Edinburgh mob was one of the fiercest in Europe. Living huddled together in the confined space of their extraordinary city, anything of importance that happened soon became their personal affair. They were quick to resent any real or supposed affront to their rights. In the congested streets a crowd formed quickly, and these crowds played a dramatic part in the city's history. With the expansion of the city and the ending of the old community of the walled town, they ceased to play the same part.

For a long period, order among this volcanic population was kept by the City Guard, mainly recruited from veteran Highland soldiers. Its duties did not make it popular. The poet Fergusson, who immortalised it as " that black banditti," gives us a vivid picture of it waging a perpetual war with the turbulent citizens, who apparently came off worst with broken heads and other injuries.

In 1726, John Porteous was appointed a Captain of the Guard. He was an unfortunate choice. A swaggering man, with a violent temper, he was proud of his friendship with the most distinguished citizens, and had an undisguised contempt for the rest. The dislike of the citizens for the Guard became concentrated on its florid captain.

In March 1736 two smugglers, Wilson and Robertson, were sentenced to death for robbing an Excise officer in Fife.

The tax levied on beer angered the Scots, and smugglers were something of popular heroes. The popularity of Wilson and Robertson was increased by a daring attempt at escape from the Tolbooth Prison. Then, three days before their execution, they were taken to the Tolbooth Church— now part of St Giles —to attend their own funeral service. The Church was packed to overflowing.

Before the service began, Robertson suddenly broke loose from his guard, and escaped through the sympathetic congregation. Wilson was held firmly by his guard, but he seized hold of the other guards and prevented them from following Robertson, who made good his escape. This increased his stock with the public enormously.

On the day of Wilson's execution, elaborate precautions were taken to prevent his rescue by the crowd. The whole City Guard was on duty, and issued with ammunition by the Provost's orders.

A detachment of soldiers was drawn up in the Lawnmarket. Porteous was furious at the presence of the soldiers, which he considered an insult to his Guard. He took his wrath out on Wilson, whom he already had a particular spite against for his part in Robertson's escape.

When Wilson was manacled to be taken to the scaffold, the manacles were found to be too small for his wrists. Porteous rushed forward and squeezed them till they shut, scoffing at Wilson's extreme pain. News of this brutality soon spread, enraging the people still more against Porteous.

The execution took place at the east end of the Grassmarket, where the Guard, expecting trouble, surrounded the scaffold. But the enormous crowd watched the ghastly ceremony in silence. Only when, twenty minutes later, the hangman began to cut down the body, did their pent-up feelings break out. Several stones were thrown at him, sending him to shelter behind the Guard.

A relative of Wilson's then rushed forward to cut down the body — to attempt to resuscitate it. No doubt to divert the Guards' attention from him, the crowd began to stone them, inflicting some injury on them.

What happened then is in doubt. Porteous was believed to have fired the first shot, killing a man. Then his men began to fire sharp dropping shots into the panic-stricken crowd. Three were killed outright, and twelve were wounded, of whom some later died. Shots fired over the crowd's heads hit spectators in nearby windows. It all happened in a few minutes. Then Porteous marched his men off.

The crowd followed, shouting angrily and throwing more stones. Half-way up the West Bow, some of the Guard turned round and fired again, killing three more and wounding others.

Few events ever caused such horror and rage in the city. It was felt that Porteous had vented his resentment and ill-nature on the crowd as he had earlier done on Wilson. The Provost and Magistrates were forced to take action. Porteous and thirty of his men were placed under arrest, and he was dismissed from his office.

The Provost and Magistrates proposed to try Porteous for murder, under their old powers to try murderers caught red-handed. One of their reasons was the well-founded fear that he would plead that the Provost had given him instructions which justified his acting as he did. For that very reason, among others, they were dissuaded from trying the case by Duncan Forbes, the Lord Advocate. On July 5, 1736, the trial of Captain Porteous opened in the High Court of Justiciary.

The indictment charged Porteous with having ordered his men to fire "without any just cause or necessary occasion." It was alleged that when some of his men fired over the heads of the crowd, he ordered them with threats to "level their pieces and be damned," and that he himself fired and killed a man.

The Crown produced twenty-eight witnesses to support their case. Porteous produced sixteen witnesses to contradict them. The jury, by a majority of one, found Porteous guilty, though they also found that several stones thrown by the crowd had injured some of his men. The correctness of the verdict has been doubted.

The crowd had given provocation, and the Provost had issued the Guard with ammunition and apparently encouraged Porteous to take a firm line. But it would have required very great provocation to justify such a terrible and indiscriminate slaughter. Moreover, his conduct towards Wilson had not been such as to avoid inciting the crowd.

The Edinburgh people had no doubt that the verdict was correct. In any case, Porteous was sentenced to death.

But Porteous had friends in high places. Many influential and aristocratic persons petitioned Queen Caroline, then ruling during the King's absence in Hanover, for his reprieve. On September 2, a reprieve reached Edinburgh.

The people of the city, who probably suspected that Porteous's rough handling of them was not regarded with entire disapproval in London, were indignant. Gradually the rumour spread that Porteous would be hanged, reprieve or no reprieve, on September 8, the day originally appointed by the Court.

The Provost hesitated to take any action. Perhaps he thought that all that was likely to happen was a spontaneous and ill-led commotion outside the Tolbooth. There were troops in the Canongate and Castle, as well as the City Guard, who could deal with that. But things turned out very differently.

In these days the city proper was still surrounded by the Flodden Wall, through which there were several gates. Outside one of these, the West Port, a small band of men assembled after nine o'clock on September 7. They seized the West Port and locked it. Then parties made off for the other gates, to seize and secure them.

At a quarter to ten, the Netherbow Port, at the foot of the High Street, was locked, shutting out the troops stationed in the Canongate.

Meanwhile, the conspirators had seized the town drum, and as they made their way through the streets the rattle of the drum brought the citizens out to join them.

A growing crowd made its way to the City Guard House in the High Street, near the Tron Church. The Guard, who had no ammunition, were soon overpowered. The rioters then made for the Tolbooth Prison, by St. Giles, where Porteous was, and began to try to batter down the door.

Of all this, the Provost and his Magistrates and other officers, spending a quiet evening in a tavern, were the last to hear. A Mr Lindsay was sent to fetch the troops in the Canongate. He was not a. magistrate, and was given no written authority. When, with difficulty, he got out of the city, he could not get the troops to act. Meanwhile, the troops in the Castle, hearing the riot, got ready to obey the summons to action which, strangely enough, never came. Naturally, after the Porteous trial, no commander was prepared to act without proper authority.

The Provost and his friends tried to intervene personally. The party which set out for the Tolbooth was twenty-six in number, but when they got there (as one Magistrate put it), "it was much smaller." No wonder! The party dissipated, and the conspirators were masters of the city.

The rioters failed to break down the Tolbooth door, so they kindled a fire and burnt it down. They had water at hand to keep the flames from spreading. Throughout, no unnecessary damage was done to persons or property.

They found Porteous calm. He asked what they wanted with him. They replied, "We are to carry you to the place where you shed so much innocent blood, and hang you." They then seized him.

Edinburgh, in its stormy history, has surely never witnessed a stranger scene than that of the excited crowd, with Captain Porteous forced along at its head in nightgown, cap and breeches, setting out unmolested to do its gruesome work, pouring up the Lawnmarket and down the West Bow by the light of flaring torches. At the Grassmarket they hanged Captain Porteous a little before midnight.

Then the crowd quietly dispersed. The Cowgate Port was opened, and many people made their way back to the country, whence they had unobtrusively come. The leaders disappeared unidentified in the crowd. It ended as quietly as it had begun. Then the dazed authorities resumed control of the city.

The reaction in London was one of astonished rage. There was perhaps less grief for Porteous than fury at the impudent defiance of the Scots. The Queen was rumoured to have said that she would "make Scotland a hunting-ground."

Reprisals were proposed against Edinburgh which resembled those inflicted on a conquered city. In the end the Government had virtually to accept defeat. The Lord Provost was made the scapegoat, and became, undeservedly, the hero of the hour.

The motives of the citizens in the riot are easy to understand. They believed Porteous to have been the murderer of innocent people, shielded by the Government in London. Used to witnessing public executions, often of criminals who had committed crimes far short of murder, the nature of their revenge probably did not appear so very extreme to them.

The mystery was, and remains, who were the daring conspirators who coolly took command of the city and conducted the riot with the skill and discipline of a military operation? The Jacobites, the Covenanters, and the smugglers were all suspected, but without definite proof.

The clergy, "those true trumpeters of sedition and cruelty in all countries," were selected as the villains of the piece. Those who might have revealed more took their secrets to the grave.

Deacon Brodie

In the Lawnmarket, a few yards above George IV Bridge, one may see the entrance to Brodie's Close. It bears the name of a prosperous family who lived there in the eighteenth century, and whose notorious son, Deacon William Brodie, may well have given R. L. Stevenson the idea for Jekyll and Hyde. For Deacon Brodie was one of the most remarkable of those men who have been pillars of society by day and dangerous criminals by night.

His father was a prosperous wright and cabinet-maker in the Lawnmarket, a Burgess, and, as Deacon of the Incorporation of Wrights, a member of the Town Council.

William Brodie went into his father's business, and prospered like him. He too became a Burgess, and, in 1781, Deacon of the Incorporation of Wrights and a member of the Town Council. He appeared to be following in his father's worthy footsteps — rich, respected, and influential in the city's affairs. On his father's death, in 1782, he inherited some valuable house property and a fortune of £10,000.

Yet for some reason Brodie was not at home in his respectable and comfortable world. Through the night the social clubs flourished, with no worries about closing hours. Brodie belonged to such a club, but his tastes led him more and more to the semi-criminal world of gamblers and cheats. Gambling became a passion with him, and he lost large sums of money. At the same time, he kept two mistresses, Anne Grant in Cant's Close, and Jean Watt in Liberton's Wynd, from both of whom he had a family.

Such a way of life would have exhausted larger fortunes. Large though his legitimate income was, Brodie had to supplement it somehow. For this he turned to burglary. As a burglar he enjoyed several advantages. His work took him into many places of business, and his social eminence took him into the houses of the well-to-do.

His great respectability protected him from suspicion. Citizens whose houses were broken into during the night never dreamed that the eminent Deacon Brodie, whom they had entertained during the evening as an honoured guest, had returned a few hours later to rob them. More likely they called him in in his professional capacity to make their houses more burglar-proof.

One old lady who awoke out of her sleep to see a masked man

rifling her bureau thought she recognised him as Deacon Brodie. So incredible was the idea that she dismissed it from her mind as nonsense, and never mentioned it to anyone until after his fall.

It is hard to imagine how anyone could lead a double life in the days when the majority of Edinburgh's citizens were still huddled together in the tall lands and crowded closes on the ridge between the Castle and Holyrood. Yet Brodie did so very successfully.

He moved about the society he preyed on, a small and rather dandified man, joining in the worried head-shaking and deliberating with his fellow Town Councillors on measures to check the recent wave of burglaries. No doubt he enjoyed the joke, for he had a good sense of humour.

Still his extravagance called for more money. His dishonest takings had so far been relatively small. To attempt larger hauls he needed accomplices. He chose three rogues from among his gambling associates—George Smith, an Englishman; Andrew Ainslie; and John Brown, alias Humphrey Moore, another Englishman, who had escaped from the law of England after being sentenced to seven years' transportation for theft.

All three, when Brodie met them, were living on their wits in the gambling dens and awaiting such an opening as he offered them. From the autumn of 1786 onwards, Brodie worked with Smith, later assuming Ainslie, and finally Brown, into the partnership.

The most interesting of their exploits was probably the theft of the silver mace of the University of Edinburgh, which they stole after breaking into the library in the Old College.

Of more importance in their career was the theft of more than £300 worth of silks and cambrics from Messrs. Inglis & Horner, silk mercers at the Cross of Edinburgh. As a result, a reward of £150 was offered for information leading to the discovery of the offenders, and the King's pardon to any accomplice who gave such information. This offer was later to bear fruit.

On March 5, 1788, Brodie's gang attempted a much more ambitious burglary, that of the General Excise Office for Scotland in the Canongate. If successful, they would reap a rich harvest there. Deacon Brodie had carried out repairs and other work in the building, and was familiar with the lay-out. In these days the keys of the offices were left hanging on a nail inside the door, and it was easy to obtain a putty impression of them.

The arrangements for guarding the premises were studied, and it was discovered that they were left unguarded between 8 o'clock, when the

office closed, and 10 o'clock, when the night watchman came on duty.

On the afternoon of the burglary, Deacon Brodie presided at a genteel little party in his comfortable home in Brodie's Close, where his sister was hostess. There he lived, for almost the last time, his public role of the eminent Burgess and man of standing.

Before eight o'clock he changed into dark clothes, put a brace of pistols and a lantern in his pocket, and set out to live his private role of criminal.

The entry into the Excise Office was easily made. Smith and Brown went to rifle the cashier's room. Brodie remained on guard just inside the main door. Ainslie crouched under a low wall which surrounded the building, to warn Brodie by whistle if anyone approached.

If Smith and Brown had found the money they sought easily, the enterprise would have been an unqualified success. But though they found some small sums here and there, a secret drawer containing £600 eluded their expert search.

While they searched, a ludicrous happening upset the enterprise. The Deputy Solicitor of Excise had left some papers in his office, and returned in a great hurry to get them.

About half-past eight Ainslie saw a man run into the courtyard and enter the Excise building, and was too surprised to warn Brodie. Brodie, standing behind the door, suddenly saw the hurried stranger enter.

If he had been warned, or had kept his head, murder might have been done. Fortunately, he completely lost his head. Pushing past the Deputy Solicitor, he rushed out of the building and took to his heels. The Deputy Solicitor assumed he was another employee who, like himself, had come to fetch something he had forgotten.

He went up to his room, found his papers, and went out, slamming the main door after him. Ainslie, who could recognise no one in the dark, had seen a man rush out of the building, and wondered what had happened. A few minutes later the mystery was deepened by the less hurried emergence of another man, who closed the door after him. It was too much for Ainslie's nerves. He, too, took to his heels.

Meanwhile, the astonished Smith and Brown inside heard the rushing to and fro, and the slamming of the door. Coming out cautiously to investigate, with pistols cocked, they found their companions gone. Cursing them for cowardly deserters, they went home.

When the four met to divide the meagre spoils, the atmosphere was charged with recrimination. Smith and Brown were particularly bitter. Brown took his share of the money, then went out and presented himself at the Sheriff Clerk's office.

The reward offered after the burglary of Inglis & Horner's shop, with its offer of a pardon to the informer, must always have tempted Brown, who had the English sentence of transportation hanging over him. After the fiasco at the Excise Office, he decided it would be more profitable to turn informer.

The next day, Ainslie and Smith were arrested. Brown had not mentioned Brodie's name. Presumably he intended to blackmail him.

Brodie's agitation on hearing of his friends' arrest can be imagined. He was desperate to know if he had been implicated. He took the bold step of going to the Tolbooth and asking to see the criminals of whose exploits he had heard so much. This request was refused.

After that his nerve failed him. He went to a cousin of his and told him the whole story. What his poor cousin felt as his relative, hitherto the ornament of their smugly respectable family, revealed his predicament, we can only guess. However, family feelings prompted him to assist the Deacon to flee from justice. Deacon Brodie escaped to London and thence to Holland.

It was Brodie's intention to go to America. But on the ship to Holland, he foolishly became friendly with a fellow-Scot, to whom he entrusted three letters, one being for his mistress, Anne Grant. This resulted in his being traced and brought back to Scotland.

The trial of Brodie and Smith opened on August 27, 1788, in the High Court of Justiciary, where, characteristically, Brodie had shortly before served as a juryman in a murder trial. Ainslie was admitted as King's evidence to corroborate Brown. A detachment of soldiers was on duty in Parliament Square to control the crowd that flocked to the Court.

Brodie was defended by the great Henry Erskine, then Dean of Faculty, and Smith by John Clerk (later Lord Eldin), who was to make his name in that case.

Brodie's mistress, Jean Watt, gave evidence that he had been with her all the night of March 5, but was not believed. The defence depended mainly on an attempt to exclude the evidence of the accomplices, Brown and Ainslie. The Court however, ruled it admissible. This led to a sensational scene.

John Clerk in his speech to the jury, told them to ignore the ruling of the Court, and advised them that they were the judges of law as well as of fact.

The Lord Justice-Clerk pointed out that he was talking nonsense. Clerk stuck to his guns replying most impertinently to the Bench, and finally refused to continue his speech unless he was allowed to have it his own way. The Lord Justice Clerk accordingly began to charge the jury. Clerk started to his feet and shook his fist at the Bench crying :"hang my client if you daur, my Lord, without hearing me in his defence." The astonished judges allowed him to continue and to repeat his unsupportable contention. No doubt in an age when people were hanged for housebreaking, defending counsel were considered entitled to such great licence.

In a splendid speech, the Dean of Faculty made the most of the evidence in support of an alibi, and threw doubt on the credibility of Brown's and Ainslie's evidence. But his case was too flimsy. The two accused were sentenced to death.

Brodie played out the last act of his career with the mocking sense of the dramatic which had marked his double life. He left a will disposing humourously of his "good and bad qualifications," including a bequest to the Lord Provost of his "political knowledge in securing Magistrates and packing corporations."

His sense of humour certainly never failed him as he waited to face, along-with his friend Smith, the punishment which to us seems so barbarously harsh. Perhaps that is why he is remembered by his city not only as one of its criminals, but also as one of its gallery of characters.

The "life" of David Haggart

In the normal course of things David Haggart, who died at the age of twenty, would soon have been forgotten. There was nothing in his career—even its final murderous act—which would lead you to think he would be written about two centuries later.

His claim to fame rests on other grounds—on the autobiography which appeared under the title, *The Life of David Haggart, alias John Wilson, alias, John Morison, alias Barney McCoul, alias John McColgan, alias Daniel O'Brien, alias The Snatcher, Written by himself while under sentence of Death.*

It professed to be the confession of a penitent sinner; but the self-laudatory tone of the work gives another impression. David Haggart obviously thought himself a great hero, and a particularly clever one. And that was how he wished the world to remember him. Above all, he was determined that the world should remember him. So, as his claims to virtue were rather slender, he set out to paint his villainies on a heroic scale.

David Haggart had stood in the dock of the High Court of Justiciary on June 11, 1821, and heard sentence of death passed on him. In his short life he had stood often in the docks of this and other Courts. Now he had been found guilty of the murder of Thomas Morrin, a turnkey, during an escape from the Tolbooth of Dumfries.

The publication of the book was arranged by his solicitor, a Mr George Robertson, W.S., who provided a foreword. In it he told how Haggart's last days were devoted partly to religious exercises and partly to furnishing material for an account of his life. He explained that the idea of the *Life* was entirely Haggart's own. It originated in a wish to atone to some degree for his crimes by disclosing them, and also to raise some money for his family and for charity.

Mr Robertson realised that Haggart's racy and boastful description of his crimes was hardly consistent with these laudable aims. But he added that, although they are described "with apparent thoughtlessness, Haggart uniformly expressed a deep sense of their enormity."

And so, with a handsome sketch of the author looking rather like Childe Harold, and at peace with the world, the book was launched.

It was an immediate success, and a second edition soon appeared. To some extent this was due to the consuming interest so many respectable people have in the lives of those who have not been respectable.

But there had been "dying confessions" before, and there have been since. David Haggart's life had merits which raised it above the common ruck of its kind. Written in a straightforward style, making use of the professional jargon of thieves and pickpockets, it was definitely readable. However deplorable the matter, the style showed some literary talent.

It did not meet with approval everywhere. *The Edinburgh Magazine* of August 1821 expressed strong doubts about "the propriety of this work ever having seen the light." It expressed anxiety about the effect on those "who hesitate between the poverty which often waits on honest industry, and the temptations of illicit gain." These warnings probably served only to boost the sales of the book.

David Haggart was born at Golden Acre, then a village near Edinburgh, on June 24, 1801. His father was a gamekeeper and dog-trainer. He did not fail in his duties as a parent, "early instructing me in religion." David got his schooling under the schoolmaster of Canon Mills, where, he admits with disarming frankness, "I was always dux of my class." At the age of ten illness made him leave school, and after that he helped his father at his work.

It was then that a "trifling accident" occurred. Fearing punishment, he determined to leave home. "From this hour," he wrote, "I date the commencement of my wicked career."

His first theft was that of a bantam cock from a lady "at the back of the New Town." The next was the theft of a till from a poor woman who kept a small shop in Stockbridge. "I knew all this was wrong," he explained. "but I took no time to be sorry or repent: and what would have been the use of repenting, for it was just all fate."

Two years later he went to Leith races and unfortunately became drunk. He sobered up to find that he had joined the army. He became a drummer in the West Norfolk Militia, stationed at Edinburgh Castle, where he met the High School boy, George Borrow, whose father was an adjutant in the Norfolks. Borrow describes him in *Lavengro*—a red-headed lad with a lithe frame, and "prodigious breadth of chest."

After a year's service, David obtained his discharge. He went back to his father, now living in the Canongate, and returned to school for a time. He obtained a post with a firm of millwrights, but soon the firm failed and he was out of work.

In the meantime, he had been keeping bad company. At the age of sixteen he chose his friends from thieves and other petty criminals, whom he often joined in their exploits. In this way he made a friendship which was to influence his life greatly. He met Barney McGuire, a youth who became his hero, and whom he describes as an Irishman, "a darling of a boy," and "a most skilful pickpocket." Barney passed on his skill to David.

David and Barney went to Portobello races in August 1817, and there David served his apprenticeship as a pickpocket. They picked out a man who was flush with money—so much so that they had to compete with "a good many old prigs," who were also edging up to him. David was there first, and dived into his "keek cloy" (breeches pocket). The haul was £11.

This was followed by various successes at fairs and races throughout the south of Scotland. A favourite strategy was for David to engage the victim in conversation while Barney picked the pocket.

Here and there David gives away his professional secrets. "Picking the suck (breast pocket)," he wrote, " is sometimes a kittle job. If the coat is buttoned, it must be opened by slipping past. Then bring the lil (pocketbook) down between the flap of the coat and the body." He made an expert's distinction between this job and that of picking a "keek cloy." He explained that he was giving this information in the public interest, to put honest people on their guard.

In the north of England, the police got on their trail. So they decided to lie low in Newcastle over Christmas and New Year.

In January 1818, they set out again. Soon afterwards, they were arrested for housebreaking. According to the law of the time, they were sentenced to death at Durham Assizes. They escaped from the prison somehow, shooting at two constables who were in pursuit, and probably killing them. Shootings of this kind were not uncommon in the days when men found guilty of housebreaking already had the noose around their necks.

With the police hot on their heels, they made their way back to Scotland. At Jedburgh, Barney was arrested for attempted theft and sentenced to prison, so David returned to Edinburgh alone.

In Edinburgh, he lodged in the Grassmarket, and tried his hand at shoplifting, housebreaking and other crimes all over the city. He fell ill and spent a period with his family, who welcomed him back and forgave him. But soon he left them again, and was in and out of jail for various crimes. By this time the police knew him and tended to arrest him on sight.

After breaking out of the Calton Jail in March 1820, David left Edinburgh again. In Dumfries, to his delight, he met Barney McGuire, and

they decided to renew their old partnership. They had high hopes of prosperous days ahead, but no sooner had they started out than Barney was "pulled" by the police, and there he disappears from the story. For, as David put it, "Poor Barney got a free passage to Botany Bay for fourteen stretch." "He was a choice spirit," he added wistfully. It was perhaps as a tribute to him that David later assumed his name for a while.

The following day, David himself was "pulled." He appeared in the High Court of Justiciary on July 12, 1820, charged with fifteen crimes, including theft, housebreaking and prisonbreaking. Before the case was heard, he had broken prison again, and the Court passed sentence of outlawry on him. After a short period on the run, he was again arrested and lodged in Dumfries Tolbooth.

With two fellow-prisoners, Dunbar and Simpson, David planned another escape. They somehow procured a file, with which they cut through their irons. Then they shouted for the turnkey, Thomas Morrin. Morrin, passing with a plate of soup for another prisoner, came unsuspectingly. David rushed at him and struck him to the floor with a stone wrapped in a piece of blanket. Dunbar assaulted him again as he lay there. Then David pulled the key from Morrin's pocket, and walked calmly to the prison door and unlocked it. Soon he was out of Dumfries and making for Carlisle.

Lying hidden in a haystack the following afternoon, David learned that he was hunted as a murderer. He heard a woman ask a boy if "that lad was taken that had broken out of Dumfries Jail." The boy answered, "No, but the jailor died last night at ten o'clock." "His words struck me to the soul," wrote David. "My heart died within me, and I was insensible for a good while: on coming to myself I could scarce believe I had heard them."

For some months, assuming various disguises, David evaded capture. He even returned to Edinburgh for a while, and went on a criminal tour of the Highlands. But eventually he found it advisable to leave Scotland. At the end of November he reached Belfast.

In Ireland he assumed an Irish brogue and tried to pass himself off as an Irishman. But the following March he was serving a sentence for attempted theft in Kilmainham Jail. There he was recognised by a Scottish police officer who was searching the Irish prisons for him and soon he was back in Scotland.

On his return to Dumfries, as he recorded with a suggestion of triumph, there were many thousands of people waiting to see him, "all crowding for a sight of Haggart the Murderer." From there he was taken to the

Calton Jail in Edinburgh.

At his trial, no evidence was led for the defence. David's counsel, Henry Cockburn, attacked Simpson, who gave evidence for the Crown, as an unreliable witness. Dunbar, the other eyewitness, had been sent to Botany Bay, evidently by an administrative error. Henry Cockburn therefore sought to show that Dunbar was the culprit. It was all that could be made of the defence. The jury, without retiring, returned a verdict of guilty.

Years later, Henry Cockburn (then Lord Cockburn) gave his impression of his client. He described him as "young, good-looking, gay, and amiable to the eye," but he added, "there was never a riper scoundrel."

Haggart pretended, at least, to take his fate philosophically, on the principle that one fated to be hanged need never fear to be drowned. But he ended his work with the hope "that this tale will show my own comrades, if ever they see it, that their wicked ways will bring them to untimely ends."

This attitude might have seemed convincing, in spite of the gusto with which Haggart's own wicked ways were described, had it not been for an added attraction at the end of the book. This was "A Sketch of the Natural Character of David Haggart, as indicated by his Cerebral Organisation," prepared by an Edinburgh lawyer who was also an amateur phrenologist. It took the form of a series of observations on the various aspects of David's character, with David's own comments on the observations.

The following is an example:—"When you became a young man, you would feel yourself superior in intellectual power, or cleverness, and discrimination, to your associates." David's comment on this was:—"I need not describe my cleverness when I became a young man, as that is well known to the public already, and to the mortification of those who were my adversaries."

Whether David intended his life to be an expression of repentance or a glorification of himself as a prince of the underworld, the result was really neither. Unwittingly, he provided the public with a study of a type of criminal whom the world of today is still trying to fathom—irresponsible, vain, convinced that he could have outwitted the world if only his luck had held, and putting the blame for it all on fate. And the picture he gives of a criminal life hardly makes it seem attractive, in spite of the *Edinburgh Magazine's* fears.

But we need not grudge David Haggart his place in the gallery of Edinburgh "characters," since, after all, it was only to the Rogues' Gallery that he aspired. The author of a *Life* that is still readable after more than 180 years has some little claim to be remembered.

Burke and Hare

On Christmas Eve, 1828, the trial of William Burke and Helen McDougall opened at the Justiciary Court in Edinburgh. It was the end of a story of murders which had horrified and angered the public, and a great crowd thronged Parliament Close seeking admission.

The story had a curious beginning. In November 1827 an old Army pensioner died a natural death at a cheap lodging-house in Tanner's Close in the West Port. Many unnatural deaths were to follow. He had owed his landlord £4. His landlord, William Hare, had heard that the teachers of anatomy paid good money for corpses for the dissecting tables. Here, surely, was a way to get some of his £4 back. He took a lodger, a ne'er-do-weel cobbler named William Burke, into his confidence. So began the Burke and Hare partnership.

After dark, the partners set out to sell their corpse. They first went to the Old College on the South Bridge, where they asked a student how to get in touch with the Professor of Anatomy. This student happened to be one of over 500 enthusiastic students who crowded the lectures of Dr Robert Knox, the most brilliant and successful of the anatomists who set up in competition with the official University teachers. So Burke and Hare were directed to Dr Knox's rooms in Surgeons' Square.

No self-respecting student would let a corpse go past his own teacher to one of the rival establishments. The law rigidly restricted the supply of bodies for dissection. The teachers, including the University professor, had to supply their dissecting tables from the Black Market.

Grave robbers—"resurrectionists"—did a profitable business. Graves were well guarded and penalties severe, but the greater the risk the greater the profit, and many bodies were stolen before they reached the grave.

Besides the professionals, the anatomy students set out at night to rob graves, like armies foraging for supplies. Battles were fought over corpses, for students made it a point of honour to see that their teachers went well supplied. But the supply never satisfied the demand. Burke and Hare were paid £7 10s. by D. Knox for their wares, and told to bring along any more they might have.

As they walked away from Surgeons' Square, they must have been thinking of the easy road to riches which had opened before them. Hare was a strong and well-built man, but sluggish, leering, and repellent. He had been a lodger in the house of which he was now master, and had been thrown out by the former landlord. The reason we can only guess. But when the landlord died Hare returned to live with the widow, who became Mrs Hare by the Scots irregular marriage. Burke, a small, neat, snub-nosed man, with sunken grey eyes, was more pleasant on the surface, but brutal and cunning beneath. He had deserted his wife and family in Ireland, and was living with a married woman, Helen McDougall. Lazy and shiftless, their discovery of the value of human flesh solved their financial worries. But robbing graves was hard work, and so alien to them.

Burke and Hare never robbed a grave. They began to prey on the living.

We can never know the full story for sure, as we are dependent on Hare's statements and Burke's confessions after conviction. But it is fairly certain that the first victims were friendless lodgers at Tanner's Close who fell ill. Burke and Hare ended their miseries and sold them to Dr Knox for £10 each. Their distinctive method was to hold their victims down and suffocate them.

But lodgers would not fall ill regularly enough. So they began to entice suitable victims to the house, destitute and helpless people whom no-one would miss. There they would ply them with drink and then murder them. Beggar women, drunks, penniless strangers, prostitutes, and anyone else decoyed by the offer of a dram, ended up on the dissecting table.

Dr Knox and his assistants paid £10 per body and asked no questions. Six pounds of this went to the Hares, as Mrs Hare took £1 for each victim murdered under her hospitable roof. One victim was accompanied by her grandson, a pitiful, dumb child of twelve. Both bodies, delivered in a herring barrel, fetched £16—and no questions asked!

No wonder the murderers grew bolder! In April 1828 they murdered Mary Paterson. She was an orphan who had grown up uncared for, and had taken to the streets. Already depraved and well known to the police at the age of eighteen, she was a girl of extraordinary beauty. It was not likely that her disappearance would be unnoticed.

Nevertheless, Mary and a companion, Janet Brown, were easily enticed by Burke to his brother's house in Gibb's Close in the Canongate, and plied with drink. Mary was soon in a drunken stupor, but Janet remained more sober. Her life was saved by the arrival of Helen McDougall, who flew into a rage of jealousy at seeing Burke with two attractive girls.

Janet departed as quickly as she could, leaving the stupefied Mary behind. She went to a friend nearby, who advised her to go and fetch Mary. But meantime the Hares had joined Burke and his mistress, and Mary was murdered in the usual way. Janet called back three times, asking for her friend, and escaped sharing her fate more by good luck than good management.

The arrival of Mary Paterson's body naturally caused some comment in Dr Knox's establishment. Several of the students knew her by sight, one knew her name, and one who had recently been in her company asked how she died. Burke said she had died of drink—a remark with some truth in it.

Murder was surely suspected, but Dr Knox and his students turned a blind eye to these little irregularities. Dr Knox's only concern was his pleasure in acquiring an anatomically perfect specimen. He had her preserved in alcohol. Janet Brown remained suspicious, but women of her profession are not in the habit of making reports to the police.

Later in that summer, Burke and Hare quarrelled. Hare had dishonestly done a little murder on the side and kept all the profits. Burke and Helen moved to a room of their own near Tanner's Close, and the quarrel was patched up. Burke's first guest at his new home was Ann McDougall, Helen's cousin by marriage, who came on a friendly visit. Her stay was brief. She fetched the usual £10.

The last but one of the murders confessed to was that of Daft Jamie. This victim was well-known and popular in Edinburgh, a big strong lad of nineteen with the mind of a child. He roamed the streets, sleeping where he found shelter and living on the kindness of sympathetic citizens.

Gentle and lovable, his disappearance would be widely noted. But he was lured to the house in Tanner's Close and murdered. He was not drunk, and fought like a tiger, engaging the full strength of Burke and Hare, who were greatly shaken by the experience, since all their other victims had been helpless. Later that day, the body arrived at Dr Knox's rooms, where it was recognised. It bore marks of the struggle Daft Jamie had made for his life. The following day Dr Knox ordered the dissection of the body to destroy the evidence.

After this bold venture, it is no wonder that Burke and Hare determined to expand their business. It was decided to establish agents in other cities, who would send bodies to Edinburgh disguised as merchandise. But over-confidence betrayed them.

On October 31, Burke saw an old woman begging in a tavern. She told him she was Irish and had come to search for her son. Her name was Mrs Docherty, and Burke claimed family relationship. Soon she was in Burke's house enjoying his hospitality.

Burke had lodgers, a Mr and Mrs Gray, staying with him and he arranged for them to go elsewhere for the night at his expense. It was Hallowe'en, and the usual merriment took place, with the Hares as guests. In the morning Mr and Mrs Gray returned and asked where the Irishwoman was. Helen McDougall said she had to throw her out for becoming too friendly with Burke.

Later in the morning, Mrs Gray went to fetch something from a heap of straw at the foot of the bed. Burke told her to keep away from there, and this, of course, aroused her curiosity. In the afternoon she found herself alone in the room with her husband, and they took the opportunity to have a look under the straw.

To their horror, they beheld the dead body of Mrs Docherty, nude and with bloodstains on the face. They took a less tolerant view than Dr Knox. They collected their possessions and made for the police station. On the way out they met Helen McDougall, who, finding what they had discovered, offered them £10 a week to keep their mouths shut. This they indignantly refused.

That evening the police arrested Burke and his mistress. They arrested the Hares on the following day. In Burke's room they found fresh blood in the straw, and a woman's clothes. They visited Dr Knox's rooms, where they found a tea chest in which was a dead body, identified by Gray as that of Mrs Docherty.

The Lord Advocate, preparing the case for the prosecution, was in a difficult position. The prosecution of Burke and Hare and their respective women was expected by the public. Yet the evidence of murder was insufficient. The method of suffocation used by the murderers left no traces of the murder, and it was possible for Mrs Docherty to have died a natural death on Hallowe'en night.

The only method of ensuring a conviction was to invite one of the murderers to become King's evidence. This role was offered to Hare, as the less dangerous of the two, and the same role had to be offered to his wife.

Of the sixteen murders we know of, Burke and his mistress were charged with the murder of Mary Paterson, Daft Jamie, and Mrs Docherty. They were represented by the leading counsel of their day. Objection was taken to the three charges in the indictment, and only the one relating to Mrs Docherty was proceeded with.

The key evidence, of course, was that of Hare. To the tense and crowded Court, the spectacle of Hare in the witness-box, cheerful and cock-sure behind the protection of the Crown, giving evidence of crime in which he himself had been a partner, must have been as bizarre as it was offensive. Hare described the murder of Mrs Docherty, assigning a strange role to himself, which he defended under cross-examination by Henry Cockburn.

Did you go out?—No.

Did you not cover your head?—No.

You stood and saw it with your own eyes?—Yes.

Did you call murder or police?—No.

Not a word?—No.

Nevertheless, his evidence secured the conviction of Burke. Helen McDougall was released on a verdict of not proven. The Court had sat all night and the jury reached its verdict at twenty past nine on Christmas morning.

On hearing the verdict, Burke looked at Helen. "Nelly," he said, "you are out of the scrape." It seems that he had genuine affection for her. He once rejected a suggestion by Mrs Hare that he should murder her and sell her to Dr Knox.

The strangest feature of the case was the failure to bring Dr Knox to justice. What had shocked the humble Grays, he had been indifferent to. In his own small way, he was a forerunner of those Nazi doctors who experimented on the victims of the concentration camps.

At length he was driven from Edinburgh by public opinion, and by that unfailing dispenser of rough justice, the Edinburgh mob, who besieged his house. The public view of his role was expressed in the still remembered verse:

> *"Up the close and doun the stair,*
> *But and ben wi' Burke and Hare.*
> *Burke's the butcher, Hare's the thief,*
> *Knox the boy that buys the beef."*

William Bennison

On Friday, July 26, 1850, a jury in the High Court of Justiciary found William Bennison guilty of bigamy and murder. To the crowd packed into the courtroom the verdict was no surprise. The evidence of guilt had been overwhelming.

Yet there followed a scene which, as the *Edinburgh Evening Courant* observed, "deepened still further the feelings of indignation and abhorrence which the trial had produced." Bennison stood up in the dock and called on Heaven to witness his innocence and to forgive the Crown witnesses their perjuries.

The public had been greatly interested in the trial. Bennison had been known among his neighbours as a good man, and a man outstanding for his religious conviction. He had been one of the pillars of a devout evangelical congregation. When such men are found to be guilty of heartless crimes, people are doubly disturbed. They feel there can be no security if even the most respectable among them may be a criminal. So they had come crowding to Parliament Square for admission and with the unfolding of the case found plenty to hold their interest.

William Bennison was born in Ireland and baptised in the Established Church. He turned away from it to religion of a more evangelical kind, and began to attend Primitive Methodist meetings.

What he looked like we must guess. But we can imagine him as rather gaunt, with the blazing eyes and intense expression of a man tormented by strong conflicting passions. For when one of the witnesses was giving evidence at the trial she suddenly stopped. She saw Bennison's eyes fixed on her, and she was unable to continue.

In 1838, Bennison married an Irish girl, Mary Mullen. They lived together for a few months and then he deserted her and came to Scotland. At Paisley he met a girl named Jean Hamilton, whom he bigamously married. She was a delicate, gentle person, who shared his religious convictions.

He was happy with her, but the existence of a lawful wife in Ireland weighed, apparently, on his mind. After a short time he left Jean and returned to Mary.

How he explained his prolonged absence we do not know. At any rate, Mary received him back, and soon he persuaded her to come to Scotland. On their arrival in Scotland, Mary died mysteriously. Bennison buried her quietly in a nameless grave, which was never traced.

Then he went back to Jean. He was in mourning, and he had some woman's clothes which he gave her. He said that they belonged to his sister, who had come over from Ireland with him and died on the journey.

Shortly afterwards, he took Jean to Ireland to visit his people. There, to her amazement, she found his only sister alive and healthy. She asked for an explanation, and was apparently satisfied with the one she received. Bennison piously explained that the woman he had spoken of was his "sister in the Lord."

Eventually the couple moved to Edinburgh, where Bennison found work. They obtained a small house in Stead's Place, near Leith Walk, where for some years they lived happily, and in 1843 a daughter was born to them. Bennison was kind and considerate. His sister-in-law, giving evidence at his trial, said that she had vowed she would respect Bennison's dust for the kindness he then showed to Jean. They became members of the Wesleyan congregation, and he threw himself wholeheartedly into its work.

In the spring of 1849, however, his affection for Jean cooled. He began to spend every evening at prayer meetings, where he found other attractions than religion in a girl called Margaret Robertson. He took long walks with her after meetings, and visited her home. Their talk turned on religious subjects, but there can be little doubt that Margaret was selected to be the third Mrs Bennison.

During the winter, Bennison spread the story that his wife's health was failing, though, in fact, she was in good health and spirits. He was preparing the ground.

About the end of February 1850, he went to the shop of William Macdonald, an apothecary, where Mrs Macdonald sold him twopence worth of arsenic. He said he needed it to kill rats.

On the evening of Friday, April 12, he made some porridge. The child was in bed, and Bennison said he was unwell and could not eat any. Jean alone took some, and on the following morning she was violently ill.

On the Saturday, a doctor was called in. He gave some ineffectual treatment. On the Sunday, Jean was much worse. She was very sick, with violent pain and great thirst. Bennison fetched Jean's sister, a Mrs Glass. According to her, his behaviour that day was "very cool." He wished some dead clothes to be looked out, and asked a woman present what sort of funeral letters he should get.

He occasionally took a look into Jean's room, but he never spoke to her or stayed to try to comfort her. In the evening, Jean asked for a doctor. Bennison said, in her hearing, that there was no use in incurring further expense. "It is no use," he said piously, "she is going home. She is going home to glory."

On the Monday morning he took a pair of black trousers to a tailor to be mended. He said he would need them if his wife died.

At one o'clock in the afternoon he returned and said she was dead. "I have seen many a death-bed," he added, "but I have never seen a pleasanter one than my wife's." She had, in fact, died about midday, in dreadful agony. Bennison was not present at the death. When told of it, he exclaimed fervently, "Thank God. She has gone to glory. She has gone home."

No sooner was Jean dead than Bennison went to live with Margaret Robertson's family. First, however, he took the wedding ring from Jean's finger. No doubt he had further use for it.

He made arrangements for the funeral to be held on the Wednesday, and accordingly consulted his minister, who thought it a little hasty. But for Bennison it could not be too hasty. Already Mrs Glass was suggesting a post-mortem examination. So he had his way.

It would have been extraordinary if Mrs Glass's suspicions had not already been aroused, and the haste in pushing forward the funeral arrangements only served to confirm them. When she had first suggested a post-mortem examination to Bennison, he was very upset. His feelings, he told her, would not stand it. "She died happy," he said. "What more could you wish?"

Mrs Glass took her suspicion to the neighbours. If they needed something more to convince them, they did not have to wait long.

With his usual carelessness, Bennison had not destroyed the remains of the poisoned porridge. Instead, he gave it to a neighbour for his dog to eat. On the same day the dog became ill, and on Tuesday morning the neighbours learned with horrified interest that it was dead. They wisely went and told their story to the Procurator-Fiscal.

Up to this point, it was possible, however highly improbable, that Bennison was innocent. His callous behaviour was not evidence of his guilt. At this point, however, like so many criminals, he completely lost his head, and supplied what was to be the last link in the evidence against him.

On Thursday, April 18, he went to see Macdonald, the apothecary. He found him in the shop with Mrs Macdonald. Bennison first told them of his wife's death and of the neighbours' suspicions. Then he mentioned the arsenic he had bought earlier in the year. Macdonald asked what he had done with it, and Bennison replied that he had given it to his wife. He said that nobody knew about it, and that the Macdonalds would be doing him a great service if they did not mention it.

He explained that there was no need for them to lie. If questioned, Macdonald could truthfully deny having sold him any arsenic, since it was, in fact, Mrs Macdonald who had done so. The Macdonalds refused to consider the suggestion.

On hearing their refusal, Bennison turned quite pale. Agitated, and with heaving breast, he burst into one of his appeals to Heaven which seemed to have so much genuine conviction in them.

"They may find the arsenic in the body," he said passionately, "but I declare to God I am innocent." He added that God had carried him through the world as yet, and he hoped He would do so still.

We can judge the conviction with which he spoke by the fact that the Macdonalds, though they considered the whole conversation "singular," were apparently satisfied when he told them that all he had done was to mix the arsenic in a plate. He said he had not seen it since. They knew Bennison's reputation as a Christian and pious man.

On Friday, April 19, on the information of the neighbours, Bennison was arrested.

At the trial, the evidence against him piled up relentlessly. His story was that he had bought the arsenic to kill rats and had given it to his wife to use. That was the last he had seen of it. He had not fetched a doctor for his wife because she would not let him.

As to the charge of bigamy, he said that when he married Jean, he believed his lawful wife, Mary, to be dead. It was a great shock when he found she was still alive. Naturally, his story was not believed.

Among other facts proved by the Crown was the fact that he had drawn £11 from various funeral benefit societies which he had thoughtfully joined.

Bennison was sentenced to death. In prison he confessed to the crimes of which he had been convicted. One cannot help wondering whether his religious fervour was, as his contemporaries believed, merely brazen hypocrisy, calculated to cloak his crimes.

Perhaps, feeling himself to be morally weak, he had clung desperately to religion, trying to find the strength he lacked, and producing only the bizarre combination of crime and religious enthusiasm which provides the interesting aspect of his character.

Although he was not charged with the murder of Mary, his lawful wife, it is impossible not to suspect him of it. Moreover, had he not been such a clumsy murderer, it is not impossible that other women would have shared Jean's fate. Indeed, Bennison might have become one of the "Bluebeards" of criminal history.

Eugene Marie Chantrelle

In 1867, Elizabeth Dyer, a pretty and headstrong girl attending a private school named Newington Academy, fell in love with one of her language teachers. He was a Frenchman named Eugene Marie Chantrelle, who had come to Edinburgh in the previous year to seek his fortune.

Chantrelle's life up till then had been rather unsettled. He was born in Nantes in 1834, the son of a prosperous and locally important family, and was given a good education. He was a brilliant student and went on to distinguish himself at Nantes Medical School.

When he was fifteen, his father lost all his money, and so Eugene had to leave the medical school and support himself. This he managed to do, and he attended medical classes in Strasbourg and Paris; but he found he could not settle down to his studies again. His medical course was never completed, and his life became restless and aimless.

In 1851, he became involved in the stormy politics of the day. To his credit, he was among those who opposed Louis Napoleon's bid for despotic power. With the success of Napoleon's coup d'état, he found it advisable to leave France.

For several years he lived in America. Then he went to England, where he taught languages for four years, at the end of which he came to Edinburgh. Here he soon became a success, teaching pupils privately and joining the staff of some of the leading schools.

He was the author of several French textbooks, which came to be used in many schools. In addition to his teaching of French and German, he was successful as a tutor in Latin and Greek. Unsettled though his life had been, he had not neglected his general education.

Chantrelle was handsome and elegant in the dandified style of his day, with a dark moustache and side-whiskers. Clever and cultured, with the polished charm of his nation, he had a cynical and disillusioned air.

With the background of his unhappy and rather mysterious past, a romantic schoolgirl of fifteen may well have seen him as a Byronic hero. It is not unnatural that Elizabeth became infatuated with him. Unfortunately for her, he became her lover, and after a few months she discovered that she was going to have a child. The effect of the news on her family can be imagined. Unhappy and bewildered, at the age of sixteen, Elizabeth was married to Chantrelle to save her reputation.

Inauspicious though this beginning was, Elizabeth tried to make her marriage happy. Sweet-natured and gentle, she was naturally a devoted wife. Chantrelle made a good income out of his teaching, and eventually the couple settled in a comfortable house in George Street. It was the perfect setting for the life of contented and rather stuffy prosperity which we imagine as the life of the comfortably off in Victorian Edinburgh.

But, within a few weeks of their marriage, Chantrelle began to subject his wife to the degrading ill-treatment which made the rest of her life miserable. He abused her continually, giving vent to the bitterness he seemed to feel over their situation. He often threatened to take her life, and once said he would give her "poison which the Faculty of Edinburgh could not detect."

Another time he threatened her with a loaded pistol. She learned to fear his threats. He often struck her, and twice she had to seek the protection of the police.

He was at home as little as possible, and then he drank continually. He was grossly and almost openly unfaithful to her, and spent a great deal of time and money in the haunts of vice which so flourished beneath the thin layer of Victorian respectability.

Elizabeth consulted a solicitor about a divorce, but could not face the public disgrace which she thought would be involved for her children and herself.

In this way the marriage dragged on miserably until New Year's Day of 1878. At that time there were three children, a boy of ten, another of seven, and a baby boy of two months. Elizabeth devoted herself to her children with the undivided affection of an unhappy wife.

Her husband's treatment of her had improved a little since he had appeared in a police court two years previously. He had then been convicted of assault on the servant girl and of threats and violence towards his wife.

But something had recently happened to make her uneasy. Her husband's debaucheries cost him large sums of money. Besides, his dissipated way of life led him to neglect his teaching, and in 1877 he found himself in debt with a dwindling income. In October of that year he insured his wife's life for £1,000, payable in the case of accidental death only.

Elizabeth did not know that he had made careful inquiries about what did and did not constitute "accidental death." But she felt that her life was in danger. Shortly before New Year she told her mother: "My life is insured now, and Mamma, you will see that my life will go soon after this insurance." One wonders if she fully realised the extent of her danger.

On New Year's Day, 1878, Elizabeth, who had always been in good health, became sick. The servant girl, who had had the day off, returned in the evening to find her mistress in bed. The baby, who always slept with his mother, was beside her. Elizabeth told the servant she had been ill but was better. The servant brought her some lemonade and peeled an orange for her, then went to bed.

Chantrelle was the last to go to his room. The two older children slept with him. So far as a bad husband can be, he seems to have been an affectionate father. He went through to his wife's room and took the baby away from her. He gave him to his eldest son to look after, because, he said, his mother needed rest.

Then he went back to his wife's room, where he spent some time before going to bed.

The following morning the servant rose about half-past six. As she went about preparing the morning tea, she heard "a moaning like a cat's." When she heard it again it occurred to her that it was coming from her mistress's room. She went in and found her moaning and unconscious.

She rushed to rouse Chantrelle, and found him awake. She told him that his wife was ill. He came through to Elizabeth's bedside, and stood there with her for a few minutes. Then suddenly he told her that he could hear the baby crying. The servant went to his room, where she found the baby fast asleep.

On entering Elizabeth's room again, she saw Chantrelle coming hurriedly away from the window. He asked her if she smelt gas, and she said she did not. Later she said that she did.

A nearby doctor, Dr Carmichael, was called in. On his arrival he was told that there had been an escape of gas in Mme. Chantrelle's room. He found her completely unconscious and very pale, and her breathing very much interrupted. There was a smell of gas in the room, though the supply had been turned off at the meter. He assumed that Elizabeth's condition was caused by gas poisoning.

In those days cases of coal-gas poisoning were very rare. He sent a card to Dr Henry Littlejohn, the City Medical Officer, who was an expert toxicologist, with the message: "Dear Sir— If you would like to see a case of coal-gas poisoning, I should like you to come up here at once."

When Dr Littlejohn came, he too assumed that it was a case of coal-gas poisoning. But it so happened that, some time before, Elizabeth had consulted Dr Littlejohn at a time when her husband's behaviour was so outrageous that she thought he must be insane. So he knew the Chantrelles' relations with each other, and he was immediately suspicious.

His suspicions were increased by Chantrelle's anxiety to impress on him, in almost the first words he spoke, that Elizabeth's state was caused by a gas escape. Dr Littlejohn had Elizabeth removed to the Royal Infirmary.

Early in the afternoon, Dr Maclagan, Professor of Medical Jurisprudence, examined the patient. Up to this time no doubt had been thrown on the assumption that it was a case of coal-gas poisoning.

After his examination, however, Dr Maclagan announced that it was not such a case. "It appears," he said, "to be a case of narcotic poisoning—possibly opium or morphia." At 4 o'clock, after some hours during which her state was barely distinguishable from that of death, Elizabeth Chantrelle died.

The following day a post-mortem examination was held. No traces of coal gas were found in the body. On the other hand, no traces of narcotic poisoning were found. But it was possible for the traces of a narcotic poison to have disappeared, while it would have been most unlikely in the case of coal gas.

Further discoveries made Chantrelle's arrest inevitable. On Mme. Chantrelle's nightdress and on some of the bedclothes were found stains which contained unmistakable traces of opium. A quantity of opium was found in a medicine chest in Chantrelle's room.

The gas was found to have escaped from a pipe behind the window shutter which had been long disused, and from which a portion appeared to have been freshly broken off.

On January 5, immediately after his wife's funeral, at which he had displayed intense grief, Chantrelle was arrested. On Tuesday, May 7, after the Crown had painstakingly built-up its case, he was brought to trial at the High Court of Justiciary, charged with his wife's murder.

So great a number of people tried to get admittance to the trial that a passage had to be cleared through the crowd for those who had to attend.

The courtroom was packed to the last seat when Chantrelle was brought in to the dock. He was in mourning, and looked pale and tired, but perfectly self-possessed. On both sides were distinguished counsel, whose forensic powers were to be fully displayed.

The Crown case was that Chantrelle had given his wife a fatal dose of opium in an orange, or in lemonade, or some other food or drink: that in the morning he sent the servant out of his wife's room on the pretext that he heard the baby crying; and that he then broke the gas pipe behind the shutter to create the impression that his wife had been poisoned by escaping gas.

This was supported by a long chain of circumstantial evidence, which was rather weak in some links, but strong in its cumulative effect. To strengthen it, evidence was led of the Chantrelles' miserable married life; of his violence, his infidelities, and his threats; and of his financial inducements to stage her "death by accident."

The defence case was mostly negative, consisting of an attempt in cross-examination to break down the Crown chain of evidence at its weaker links. A strong point was made of the fact that the first two doctors in the case had at first accepted it as a case of coal-gas poisoning.

At times the medical witnesses were shaken by the cross-examination, but the defence could not discredit them.

When the long case for the Crown closed, the defence called very few witnesses. Of these, most gave evidence that Chantrelle had given them medical treatment. He had, in fact, carried on a sort of medical practice purely for the purpose of saving people from the hands of the medical profession, for which he professed a distrust. That could account for his possession of opium.

When the defence case closed, Chantrelle's composure was disturbed for the first time during the trial. He was shocked by the slenderness of his case. The people who crowded the courtroom heard him ask his counsel reproachfully, "Is that ALL the evidence for the defence?"

At the end of a four days' trial, Chantrelle was found "Guilty of murder as libelled," and sentenced to death. He protested his innocence to the end.

Public interest had grown to an intense pitch as the four days' evidence unfolded the story of that ill-starred marriage. Elizabeth Chantrelle had not sought the divorce or separation which would have saved her life, because she did not want to make public the sordid details of her unhappy existence with her husband.

Yet at the trial these very details were painstakingly brought to light, before an intensely interested public, to prove that she had died at his hands the death she had so long feared. It gave a strangely ironic ending to the tragedy.

"Antique" Smith, forger

For some years in the 1880s a quiet-mannered and undistinguished-looking man could frequently be seen browsing among the second-hand bookshops on George IV Bridge. The books he seemed to be hunting for were any that looked old and had large fly-leaves. These he bought, whatever the contents, and carried them off himself, refusing any offer to have them sent to his home.

To the people in the shops he no doubt appeared to be just another of Edinburgh's eccentrics. It could not occur to them till much later that they were seeing one of Edinburgh's most curious criminals collecting the raw materials for his trade—the large-scale forging of literary and historical documents.

The industry of this unobtrusive man filled the market for several years with spurious letters and poems by Burns and Scott, supposed Jacobite documents and other manuscripts which found their way into the hands of collectors.

The extraordinary thing is that he was able to carry on this kind of fraud for so long. No doubt this kind of forger enjoys, like the confidence man, a peculiar protection. As often as not his victim is reluctant to expose him. When an expert accepts a crude forgery as the genuine article, he often prefers to bear his financial loss in silence and save his reputation. If he has published his prize, thinking it to be genuine, he will fiercely defend it against any attacks.

With so many of these spurious documents on the market, some public controversies were bound to arise. When, in 1891, a Mr Mackenzie sold a collection known as the Rillbank Crescent Manuscripts by auction, the auctioneer began by announcing that the genuineness of the manuscripts had been called into question. They were, he said, offered for sale as genuine, but the purchasers must make up their own minds. Naturally, they did not fetch record prices. What is surprising is that they fetched anything at all.

Shortly afterwards the same Mr Mackenzie published in the Press a "hitherto unpublished" letter by Burns to a friend, "John Hill, weaver, Cumnock." Certain experts attacked the letter as spurious. Certainly it proved impossible to find any trace of John Hill ever having existed. But Mr Mackenzie replied vigorously to this attack and claimed to be supported by a most distinguished expert.

The expert proved to be Mr James Stillie, an Edinburgh bookseller who dealt largely in Burns manuscripts and had known Sir Walter Scott. He was certainly an authority of some standing locally. He publicly announced his opinion that the letter was genuine.

Mackenzie followed up the letter with a "hitherto unpublished" poem by Burns, entitled "To a Rosebud," and beginning, "All hail to thee, thou bawmy bud." This also he defended against the hostile critics.

Finally, he published two more poems by Burns from his collection. The publication of hitherto unpublished poems by Burns aroused some public interest. Unfortunately for Mr Mackenzie, his critics managed to prove that the two poems had appeared in the works of other authors some years before Burns had begun to write, let alone publish, any poetry. A little later Mr Mackenzie retired from the field.

Mr James Stillie himself became involved in a dispute which showed how far afield the forged manuscripts had circulated. He had sold a collection of manuscripts, many allegedly written by Burns, for the sum of £750.

The purchaser was a Mr Kennedy, a wealthy American who had hoped to present the collection to a New York library. However, some public controversy regarding similar documents aroused his suspicions. He accordingly submitted the collection to the British Museum experts, who declared them all, with one exception, to be obvious forgeries. Mr Kennedy therefore demanded his money back.

But Mr Stillie had a great contempt for English experts, some of whom had recently declared a collection which he had sold to an English customer to consist entirely of forgeries. So he refused to return Mr Kennedy's money.

The prevalence of documents of doubtful authenticity was thus becoming a scandal which involved the reputation of Scottish dealers outside Scotland.

But the documents continued to flood on to the market, until the *Edinburgh Evening Dispatch* took steps to expose the affair.

On November 22, 1892, the *Dispatch* began a series of articles bringing the question to the notice of the public. It was pointed out that the matter was one of national concern. With the articles were published facsimiles of some forged manuscripts which a well-known Edinburgh bookseller had bought at a sale. One reader recognised the writing of the facsimiles as being similar to that of a copying clerk whom he casually employed.

In this way, the *Dispatch* articles led to the discovery that the spurious documents had been fabricated by Alexander Howland Smith, a clerk in his early thirties, who was known to his friends as "Antique" Smith because of his preoccupation with old books and documents. He was visited by a *Dispatch* reporter, to whom he explained that he had put many literary and historic documents on the market.

Smith said he had been at one time clerk to the late Thomas Ferrier, Writer to the Signet. Mr Ferrier had once told him to destroy some old papers which were piled almost knee-high in his office.

Smith took them home, and, as Mr Ferrier's father had been agent to several important people, many of the papers proved to be of great interest. He sold them from time to time, and when the supply was finally exhausted he forged some more.

Year after year, Smith had worked away at his documents in a little summer-house behind Hope Crescent in Leith Walk.

On December 5, Smith was arrested. In the meantime, the Dispatch continued to publish articles on the subject of the forgeries, in which it omitted all mention of Smith's name, but continued to comment on the forgeries generally. On December 17, on the petition of Smith, the High Court of Justiciary ordered the *Dispatch* to cease publishing articles on the subject until the end of his trial, though, in his judgment, the Lord Justice-Clerk paid tribute to the public service which the *Dispatch* had performed in bringing the matter of the forgeries to light.

On June 26, 1893, Smith was charged in the High Court with "fabricating manuscripts or other documents of apparent historic or literary interest" and fraudulently disposing of them as genuine.

The Crown case opened with the evidence of Andrew Brown, a bookseller in Bristo Place. For him the experience must have been extremely embarrassing. He explained that Smith had first come to his shop in 1886, when he sold him an album of the autographs of several famous men.

Smith had explained that he had obtained his documents from Mr Ferrier's office. Brown had visited Mr Ferrier to verify the story, and Ferrier had told him that it was possible there were some such documents in his office. After that, however, Brown had accepted so many documents from Smith that it was impossible he could have believed them all to be genuine.

Smith's counsel attempted to attack Brown's evidence on that ground. But it was a fruitless line of attack, since it involved virtual accept-

ance of the prisoner's guilt and put the defence in a hopelessly contradictory position.

Other Crown witnesses included a pawnbroker with whom Smith had pawned some manuscripts. The pawnbroker accepted the manuscripts as genuine, but was suspicious of Smith. He asked him how he had come by the documents. Smith had shown him a will by Mr Ferrier, bequeathing the manuscripts to hin. Needless to say, the will, too, was forged.

The Crown called two witnesses who gave expert evidence to prove the manuscripts spurious. This evidence revealed the astonishing crudity of some of the forgeries. Certain letters were written on fly leaves torn out of books. One was written on a piece of paper which was worm-eaten, and the writer had taken care to avoid the worm holes.

In one document, which had been sold as an unpublished poem by Burns in the poet's handwriting, the poem was taken from the works of Pope. Two letters by Burns to different persons had the same contents, word for word. In another letter the signature of Robert Burns had clearly been written in pencil and inked over.

Letters by Lord Macaulay and James Watt were found to have been written in a hand which bore no resemblance to theirs. In fact, the writing on all the documents was that of the same person, and in some cases the same paper had been used for documents of various periods.

The evidence for the defence consisted of that of Smith's sister, who said that she saw him take papers home from Mr Ferrier's office; and the evidence of a person who lived with him for some time, and had never seen him at work on any forgery. Smith was found guilty and sentenced to twelve months' imprisonment.

It is not hard to sympathise with the attitude of the jury, who recommended leniency because of the unusual character of the crime and the facility afforded Smith for disposing of the spurious manuscripts.

When several dealers and collectors were prepared to accept such palpable forgeries as genuine Smith was certainly faced with a very great temptation.

He is a curious figure in the history of crime, prowling about the second-hand bookshops in search of books with large fly leaves, or sitting in his summer-house, industriously working away at the crude forgeries which found their way through Scotland and England and abroad to the United States and elsewhere.

One wonders whether he ever saw the oddity of the situation.

Edinburgh bestsellers from Lang Syne

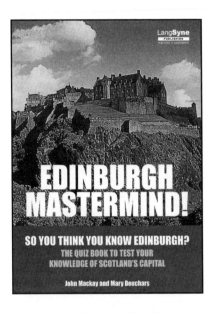

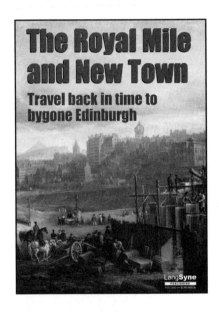

EDINBURGH MASTERMIND!

So you think you know Edinburgh?
Test your knowledge with this quiz
book.

£4.99
ISBN 1-85217-190-1

THE ROYAL MILE AND NEW TOWN

A fascinating account of the people,
places and events that helped to
shape our beautiful capital.

£5.99
ISBN 0-946264-92-9

Lang**Syne**

PUBLISHING

WRITING *to* REMEMBER

Edinburgh bestsellers from Lang Syne

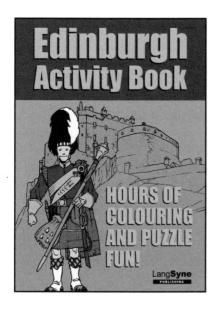

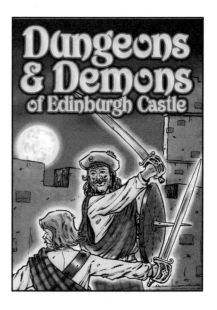

EDINBURGH ACTIVITY BOOK

Greyfriars Bobby and other Edinburghstories and places provide hours of fun.

£2.99
ISBN 1-85217-105-7

DUNGEONS & DEMONS OF EDINBURGH CASTLE

Murder and torture, magic and witchcraft, kidnappings, sieges and sabotage.

£2.99
ISBN 1-85217-149-9

LangSyne
PUBLISHING
WRITING *to* REMEMBER